Child

Opposing Viewpoints®

Abuse

OTHER BOOKS OF RELATED INTEREST

OPPOSING VIEWPOINTS SERIES

Abortion

Adoption

American Values

Child Welfare

The Family

Media Violence

Pornography

Sexual Violence

Teens at Risk

Welfare

Working Women

CURRENT CONTROVERSIES SERIES

The Abortion Controversy

Family Violence

Marriage and Divorce

Violence Against Women

Violence in the Media

Youth Violence

AT ISSUE SERIES

Child Labor and Sweatshops

Child Sexual Abuse

Domestic Violence

Single-Parent Families

CONTEMPORARY ISSUES COMPANION SERIES

Battered Women

Child

Opposing Viewpoints®

Abuse

David L. Bender, *Publisher*
Bruno Leone, *Executive Editor*
Bonnie Szumski, *Editorial Director*
Brenda Stalcup, *Managing Editor*
Scott Barbour, *Senior Editor*
Jennifer Hurley, *Book Editor*

OPPOSING
VIEWPOINTS®
SERIES

Greenhaven Press, Inc., San Diego, California

Cover photo: Craig MacLain

Library of Congress Cataloging-in-Publication Data

Child abuse : opposing viewpoints / Jennifer A. Hurley, book editor.
    p.   cm. — (Opposing viewpoints series)
Includes bibliographical references and index.
ISBN 1-56510-935-X (lib. bdg. : alk. paper). —
ISBN 1-56510-173-1 (pbk. : alk. paper)
  1. Child abuse—United States. 2. Child abuse—Investigation
—United States. 3.Child molesters—United States. I. Hurley, Jennifer
A., 1973– . II. Series: Opposing viewpoints series (Unnumbered)
HV6626.52.C545 1999
362.76'0973—dc21   98-16387
                                     CIP

Greenhaven Press, Inc., P.O. Box 289009
San Diego, CA 92198-9009

"CONGRESS SHALL MAKE NO LAW... ABRIDGING THE FREEDOM OF SPEECH, OR OF THE PRESS."

First Amendment to the U.S. Constitution

The basic foundation of our democracy is the First Amendment guarantee of freedom of expression. The Opposing Viewpoints Series is dedicated to the concept of this basic freedom and the idea that it is more important to practice it than to enshrine it.

CONTENTS

WHY CONSIDER OPPOSING VIEWPOINTS?

> "The only way in which a human being can make some approach to knowing the whole of a subject is by hearing what can be said about it by persons of every variety of opinion and studying all modes in which it can be looked at by every character of mind. No wise man ever acquired his wisdom in any mode but this."
>
> John Stuart Mill

In our media-intensive culture it is not difficult to find differing opinions. Thousands of newspapers and magazines and dozens of radio and television talk shows resound with differing points of view. The difficulty lies in deciding which opinion to agree with and which "experts" seem the most credible. The more inundated we become with differing opinions and claims, the more essential it is to hone critical reading and thinking skills to evaluate these ideas. Opposing Viewpoints books address this problem directly by presenting stimulating debates that can be used to enhance and teach these skills. The varied opinions contained in each book examine many different aspects of a single issue. While examining these conveniently edited opposing views, readers can develop critical thinking skills such as the ability to compare and contrast authors' credibility, facts, argumentation styles, use of persuasive techniques, and other stylistic tools. In short, the Opposing Viewpoints Series is an ideal way to attain the higher-level thinking and reading skills so essential in a culture of diverse and contradictory opinions.

In addition to providing a tool for critical thinking, Opposing Viewpoints books challenge readers to question their own strongly held opinions and assumptions. Most people form their opinions on the basis of upbringing, peer pressure, and personal, cultural, or professional bias. By reading carefully balanced opposing views, readers must directly confront new ideas as well as the opinions of those with whom they disagree. This is not to simplistically argue that everyone who reads opposing views will—or should—change his or her opinion. Instead, the series enhances readers' understanding of their own views by encouraging confrontation with opposing ideas. Careful examination of others' views can lead to the readers' understanding of the logical inconsistencies in their own opinions, perspective on why they hold an opinion, and the consideration of the possibility that their opinion requires further evaluation.

EVALUATING OTHER OPINIONS

To ensure that this type of examination occurs, Opposing Viewpoints books present all types of opinions. Prominent spokespeople on different sides of each issue as well as well-known professionals from many disciplines challenge the reader. An additional goal of the series is to provide a forum for other, less known, or even unpopular viewpoints. The opinion of an ordinary person who has had to make the decision to cut off life support from a terminally ill relative, for example, may be just as valuable and provide just as much insight as a medical ethicist's professional opinion. The editors have two additional purposes in including these less known views. One, the editors encourage readers to respect others' opinions—even when not enhanced by professional credibility. It is only by reading or listening to and objectively evaluating others' ideas that one can determine whether they are worthy of consideration. Two, the inclusion of such viewpoints encourages the important critical thinking skill of objectively evaluating an author's credentials and bias. This evaluation will illuminate an author's reasons for taking a particular stance on an issue and will aid in readers' evaluation of the author's ideas.

As series editors of the Opposing Viewpoints Series, it is our hope that these books will give readers a deeper understanding of the issues debated and an appreciation of the complexity of even seemingly simple issues when good and honest people disagree. This awareness is particularly important in a democratic society such as ours in which people enter into public debate to determine the common good. Those with whom one disagrees should not be regarded as enemies but rather as people whose views deserve careful examination and may shed light on one's own.

Thomas Jefferson once said that "difference of opinion leads to inquiry, and inquiry to truth." Jefferson, a broadly educated man, argued that "if a nation expects to be ignorant and free . . . it expects what never was and never will be." As individuals and as a nation, it is imperative that we consider the opinions of others and examine them with skill and discernment. The Opposing Viewpoints Series is intended to help readers achieve this goal.

David L. Bender & Bruno Leone,
Series Editors

Greenhaven Press anthologies primarily consist of previously published material taken from a variety of sources, including periodicals, books, scholarly journals, newspapers, government documents, and position papers from private and public organizations. These original sources are often edited for length and to ensure their accessibility for a young adult audience. The anthology editors also change the original titles of these works in order to clearly present the main thesis of each viewpoint and to explicitly indicate the opinion presented in the viewpoint. These alterations are made in consideration of both the reading and comprehension levels of a young adult audience. Every effort is made to ensure that Greenhaven Press accurately reflects the original intent of the authors included in this anthology.

INTRODUCTION

"There are far more children brutalized than we know about."
—Anne Cohn Donnelly

"Abuse cases, in which children suffer physical injuries, are actually very rare."
—Rachel L. Swarn

Most people would agree that as long as children are subject to neglect, mistreatment, sexual abuse, or murder, child abuse should be considered a serious problem. Debate has ensued, however, over the scope of this problem. Because reports on the prevalence of child abuse vary, parents and policy makers are not sure whether to regard the issue with concern or with panic. The prevalence of child abuse is difficult to pinpoint for two reasons: Incidents of abuse are sometimes never reported, and of the incidents that are reported, some may be false.

A number of social commentators argue that child abuse is a far more serious problem than the general public believes. The number of cases of child abuse rose substantially during the early 1990s, with one government study stating that the number of reported cases of child abuse and neglect doubled from 1.4 million in 1986 to 2.8 million in 1993. Yet some say that these figures still do not reflect the frequency with which child abuse occurs. Those who believe that the incidence of child abuse is underestimated point out that child protective service agencies often fail to pursue child abuse accusations, and when they do formally charge an alleged abuser, prosecutors do not usually bring the abuse case to trial. According to the National Center for Prosecution of Child Abuse, "Over 90% of child sexual abuse cases presented to prosecutors do not go to trial. Over half are not charged or dropped after charging."

Furthermore, those who hold that child abuse is underreported assert that child sexual abuse is far more common than most people realize, with some research estimating that close to one in four American girls are victims of sexual abuse. According to these commentators, many people are unwilling to believe that child sexual abuse is prevalent due to the horrendous nature of the crime. As Jennifer J. Freyd states, "Disbelief [about the prevalence of child sexual abuse] may . . . reflect the difficulty most of us have in thinking that adults—especially good-looking, middle-class adults—would be motivated to engage in sexual behavior with children."

Others maintain that the occurrence of child abuse, particularly child sexual abuse, is actually quite rare. They attribute the growing number of accusations of child sexual abuse in preschools to a hysterical mentality about child abuse—a mentality that has often been compared to the infamous Salem witchhunt in the late 1600s, during which twenty Massachusetts women were executed for being "witches." A media frenzy about child sexual abuse, some claim, has incited fear to the point that all accusations of abuse are assumed to be true. Furthermore, a number of social critics assert that child sexual abuse allegations often spring from the vivid imaginations of very young children, whose accusations of abuse are encouraged by parents or therapists.

An example of children's imaginations gone awry, say some commentators, is the case of Kelly Michaels. A twenty-two-year-old day care worker at the Wee Care Nursery School in New Jersey, Michaels was accused in 1985 of sexually abusing twenty preschoolers. Skeptics of the charges contend that the allegations were obviously the product of children's overactive imaginations; they note that among other things, Michaels was charged with "licking peanut butter off of [children's] genitals, . . . assaulting them with silverware, a sword, and Lego blocks . . . [and] amputating children's penises." A jury convicted Michaels of 114 counts of assault, sexual abuse, and terroristic threats—charges that were overturned in 1993, but not before Michaels had spent five years in prison. Many commentators believe that accusations such as these are inspired by the public's irrational panic about child sexual abuse—a panic that only encourages more fantastical accusations, thereby ruining the lives of innocent people.

However, those who believe child abuse is extremely prevalent say that when it comes to protecting children from abuse, it is impossible to be too careful. They assert that the experience of sexual abuse is so traumatic that child victims often retract their accounts of abuse or say what they believe interviewers want to hear—neither of which means that the abuse did not occur. Moreover, some commentators claim, heinous acts of sexual abuse happen frequently enough to justify real concern. As proof they cite a 1995 Gallup poll that estimates that 1.3 million children are victims of sexual abuse each year.

Policies designed to prevent child abuse and punish abusers are often influenced by these competing views about the prevalence of child abuse. Those who believe child abuse is extremely prevalent push for a more aggressive child protection system that would allow charges to be investigated and prosecuted more efficiently. On the other hand, those who maintain that child abuse is overestimated argue that the authority of the child protection system should be limited so as to prevent frivolous investigations. *Opposing Viewpoints: Child Abuse* examines the controversies surrounding the issue of child abuse in the following chapters: What Causes Child Abuse? Are False Allegations of Child Sexual Abuse a Serious Problem? How Should the Legal System Deal with Child Molesters? How Can Child Abuse Be Reduced? In discussing these controversies, the authors included in this anthology address the difficult challenge of safeguarding children in a world that can be perilous.

WHAT CAUSES CHILD ABUSE?

CHAPTER PREFACE

In a case that eventually went to the North Dakota Supreme Court, the state's Department of Human Services charged in 1994 that Jim and Kim Raboin had committed child abuse in disciplining their six children by spanking them with wooden spoons and leather belts. Reversing prior rulings, the Supreme Court of North Dakota determined in its 1996 decision that since the spankings did not inflict physical or mental harm on the children, they did not constitute child abuse.

The court's verdict, however, has been criticized by child welfare advocates who oppose the practice of corporal punishment under any circumstance. Opponents of spanking contend that the use of physical discipline is dangerous because it often escalates into child abuse. When spanking fails to achieve its desired results, they claim, parents often increase the intensity, sometimes inflicting injury upon the child. Moreover, argue opponents of corporal punishment, some studies have determined that disciplinary spanking makes children more prone to becoming abusive parents themselves. Researcher Murray A. Straus maintains that "society as a whole, not just children, could benefit from ending the system of violent child-rearing that goes under the euphemism of spanking."

Advocates of corporal punishment, on the other hand, blame the attack on spanking on an irrational hysteria about child abuse. Some critics fault an overzealous child protection system for this hysteria, alleging that social workers are quick to confuse incidents of physical discipline with those of abuse. In reality, advocates of corporal punishment contend, spanking is a safe and effective means of disciplining children. Proponents of disciplinary spanking cite a study conducted at Northwestern University Medical School that describes the effects of corporal punishment as beneficial, not detrimental. In addition, a 1995 government report from Sweden revealed that since corporal punishment was outlawed in that country, child abuse has risen dramatically—a finding that leads some researchers to conclude that responsible disciplinary spanking actually reduces the incidence of child abuse.

Controversy remains over whether spanking is an effective form of discipline or a punishment with deleterious effects. The following chapter discusses corporal punishment and other potential causes of child abuse.

| "Cohabitation seems to be the biggest culprit in fostering the subculture of child abuse."

THE DISINTEGRATION OF FAMILY VALUES IS RESPONSIBLE FOR CHILD ABUSE

Patrick F. Fagan

Citing a study that examines the relationship between family structure and child abuse, Patrick F. Fagan alleges in the following viewpoint that married parents are the least likely to be abusive to their children. Furthermore, claims Fagan, single-parent and other nontraditional families are prone to instability, poverty, and violence—traits that lead to a "subculture of abuse." Fagan is William H.G. Fitzgerald Senior Fellow of the Heritage Foundation, a conservative public policy research institute.

As you read, consider the following questions:
1. According to Fagan, what environments cause higher rates of child abuse?
2. In the author's opinion, why does growing up with cohabiting couples put children at risk?
3. What does Fagan believe are the most likely causes of child abuse by a mother?

Reprinted from Patrick F. Fagan, "The Child Abuse Crisis: The Disintegration of Marriage, Family, and the American Community," *Backgrounder*, June 3, 1997, by permission of The Heritage Foundation.

Something is seriously and deeply wrong with a society that has lost its ability to foster stable environments—especially two-parent families with married biological parents—within which children are loved and protected. The barometer of this failing is a vicious one: the increasing abuse of children and the related increase in violent crime.

Typically, the tendency has been to blame poverty for this increase, but there is more to the picture of child abuse in the United States. Research on the homeless and welfare recipients has found that over 40 percent of homeless mothers and housed welfare mothers were sexually molested at least once before they reached adulthood; nearly two-thirds of the overall sample were subjected to severe physical assault by an intimate as adults. . . .

DATA ON FAMILY STRUCTURE AND CHILD ABUSE

A study conducted by the Family Education Trust in Great Britain meticulously explored the relationship between particular types of family structure and abuse, accumulating clear data on family configuration in actual cases of abuse from 1982 to 1988. The results of this study shed light on a pattern that is highly correlated with child abuse today in both England and the United States: the absence of marriage and the presence of cohabitation.

The evidence from Great Britain is especially significant because, to date, this is the only study to explore the relationship between family structure and abuse. Specifically:

- The safest environment for a child—that is, the family environment with the lowest risk ratio for physical abuse—is one in which the biological parents are married and the family has always been intact.
- The rate of abuse is six times higher in the second-safest environment: the blended family in which the divorced mother has remarried.
- The rate of abuse is 14 times higher if the child is living with a biological mother who lives alone.
- The rate of abuse is 20 times higher if the child is living with a biological father who lives alone.
- The rate of abuse is 20 times higher if the child is living with biological parents who are not married but are cohabiting.
- The rate of abuse is 33 times higher if the child is living with a mother who is cohabiting with another man.

According to the British data, similar risks apply in cases of fatal child abuse. The overwhelming number of child deaths occurred in households in which the child's biological mother was cohabiting with someone who was unrelated to the child.

MARRIED PARENTS ARE THE LEAST LIKELY TO ABUSE

In Britain, a child whose biological mother cohabits was 33 times more likely to suffer serious abuse than a child with married parents

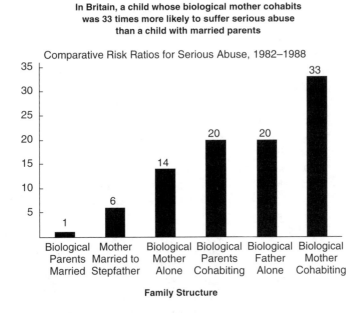

Comparative Risk Ratios for Serious Abuse, 1982–1988

Robert Whelan, *Broken Homes & Battered Children*, 1993.

Cohabitation increases the risk of child abuse immensely, whether the biological parents are cohabiting or the mother is cohabiting with a boyfriend. Both conditions rank very high on the risk scale, but the environment in which a child lives with the mother's cohabiting boyfriend is by far the worst.

Although the marriage of biological parents does not guarantee childhood happiness and security, as the presence of child abuse in these families attests, children are still safest in a married household. Furthermore, an adult decision not to marry but to live with someone out of wedlock provides the most dangerous family configuration for children. Although the most current evidence for this comes from the British study, the situation is more than likely the same in the United States. . . .

THE HIGH-ABUSE COMMUNITY

Americans today are gravely concerned about two great problems: the breakdown of traditional institutions and the deterioration of the country's inner cities. Dangerous trends, including a rise in violent crime involving younger and younger children and a resurgence of drug abuse and addiction, afflict communities throughout the country. On top of this, there has been an alarming increase in the amount and intensity of serious child abuse. The subculture of abuse, once hidden behind closed doors, is visible in the breakdown of the institutions that strengthen community.

Some communities have much higher rates of child abuse than others. In these communities, marriage is less common, individual families are more isolated, alcohol abuse is widespread, and drug trafficking is high. Although men who are abusive tend to be so whether drunk or sober, the abuse is more predictable when they are drunk. There is an acceptance among men in high-abuse communities that abusing women is normal, even condoned. As the poverty and family structure data illustrate, family income in these communities generally is less than $15,000 per year. In addition, vacant housing and transience are high.

UNSTABLE "FAMILIES"

Within these communities, stable marriages are being replaced by unstable "families" characterized by frequent changes of partners. For a mother, this results in greater stress and isolation from family and neighbors. Frequent family changes also result in frequent role changes for adults in the household, leading to more confusion and more stress for the entire family. The neighborhood has an increasing number of third- and fourth-generation out-of-wedlock children who are in poorer health, have lower levels of education and intelligence, achieve less success in school and on the job, and exhibit rising rates of drug addiction, crime, welfare dependence, and out-of-wedlock teen births. There is evidence in the National Longitudinal Survey of Youth, conducted by the U.S. Departments of Labor and Health and Human Services, that these patterns are compounding from generation to generation.

Professor Jill Rosenbaum, Professor of Criminology at California State University, Fullerton, described the family life of a typical female delinquent in 1980:

> In 1980, records were requested on 240 women who had been committed to the California Youth Authority (CYA), the state agency for juvenile offenders. . . . Very few (seven percent) of these girls came from intact homes families. . . . By the time these girls were 16, their mothers had been married an average of four times, and there was an average of 4.3 children per fam-

ily . . . 76 percent of the girls came from families where there was a record of criminality . . . violence was present in many of these homes. . . .

In the two parent families (mainly step families) . . . a great deal of conflict was present. Of these parents, 71 percent fought regularly about the children. . . . Conflict over the use of alcohol was present in 81 percent of the homes. . . . Many of the girls received very little positive feedback from parents in the home. Of the fathers who were present, 53 percent were viewed by parole officers as rejecting of the girl, as were 47 percent of the mothers. Rejection came in many forms. . . . The mothers appeared to be not only neglectful, but 96 percent were described as passive and 67 percent as irresponsible. . . .

The mothers of the CYA wards tend to marry young, with 44 percent having had the ward by the time she was 18. These daughters tended to follow in their mothers' footsteps and begin bearing children at an early age. . . . Parents often encouraged this behavior. . . . The mothers of the CYA girls did not know how to be mothers, for they were often children themselves when their children were born, and lacked the emotional resources to instill a sense of trust and security necessary for self-esteem and growth. Over time, just trying to survive depleted whatever emotional resources they might once have had.

In the 17 years since this research was conducted, another generation of abused and neglected children has grown up in these conditions. In sharp contrast, the professional literature documents and reinforces what ordinary Americans would expect: that tranquillity and peace in the family and in the marriage help prevent delinquency.

THE ABUSING FAMILY

Today, more Americans live in a manner that separates the bearing and raising of children from traditional marriage. This undermines the well-being of children. In 1950, for every 100 children born in the United States, 12 entered broken families, either by being born out of wedlock or through their parents' obtaining a divorce that year. In 1992, for every 100 children born in the United States, 60 entered broken families. The picture is even worse if all the children who are aborted each year are taken into consideration. The United States increasingly is becoming a country of second-, third-, and even fourth-generation marriage-less "families." In such circumstances, as the research shows, children are most likely to suffer abuse and neglect, and new subcultures of abuse are more likely to be established.

For example, the British study shows that a child is safest when his biological parents are married and least safe when his mother is cohabiting. In between these two poles are rising rates of abuse for the different family configurations. U.S. studies also indicate a significant difference in risk depending on whether the child's mother is married to the biological father or to a stepfather. Children with stepparents are at higher risk for both physical and sexual abuse.

According to the professional literature, an abusing family tends not to be the traditional American family—that is, one in which the biological parents are married and raising their own children together. Members of an abusing family often fight over infidelity, and the primary parent frequently will change partners, causing stressful rearrangements of major family responsibilities and conflicts over the children. Other characteristics of these families include poor communication skills, inappropriate expectations of their children, and frequent alcohol and drug abuse. Occasionally the patterns of abuse documented in the professional literature are revealed dramatically in actual occurrences. A 1996 article in the *Washington Post* illustrates how cohabitation can relate to child abuse and the death of a child:

> On the night Bridgette was killed it was the child's "sighing" that upset her father's girlfriend, then 20 and a student [who] was studying for an exam. After failed attempts to quiet the child, Davis watched as Meridin, who is not the child's mother, pushed Bridgette's forehead with her finger, picked the child up by her head and flung her toward him. Then he and Meridin stuffed a pair of socks into Bridgette's mouth, placed a hooded sweat shirt backward around the child's head and secured it with duct tape. Bridgette then was placed in a closet and partially covered with clothes. Meanwhile, Davis and Meridin sat down to eat dinner.

Growing up is much more dangerous with cohabiting couples. So are fights about infidelity and jealousy, a characteristic that may well be key in identifying the abusing family. Less able to talk through differences and difficulties and come to agreement, cohabiting couples frequently use force and aggression. "Normal" and stable families, on the other hand, typically exhibit a high level of agreement between parents and strong affection between parents and children, both of which result in much greater levels of agreement between adolescents and their parents. In addition, there is evidence that stable families participate at a higher rate in religious worship. Abuse can be tied to poverty, community, and marital status, even though not all poor, single, inner-city parents become abusers.

ABUSIVE MEN AND WOMEN

According to the studies, a boy severely abused by his father is very likely to become a violent adult. Men who have witnessed their parents, or a parent and cohabiting non-parent, physically attack each other are three times as likely to hit their own wives or cohabiting females. Moreover, the effects of these early experiences with abuse and violence begin to show up at the beginning of their relationships with women in later years. Many of the background characteristics of wife-batterers exist in college men who engage in low-level courtship violence. Growing concerns about date rape should lead investigators to explore the early family histories of abusing males in more detail.

For abusing men, violence frequently is a way to regain what they see as their lost control of a relationship. Conflict over children is likely to provoke this sense of a loss of control, and even to lead a couple to blows.

Contrary to public perception, research shows that the most likely physical abuser of a young child will be that child's mother, not a male in the household, although the mother's plight often is complicated by her relationship with a cohabiting male. Abusive mothers frequently are isolated, and lack the parental and extended family or peer support that is necessary to maintain their self-esteem and to buffer the stress of raising children. Without this support, they often seek care and comfort from their children, treating these children as if they were older than they really are. When children fail to provide this support, the mother can become impatient, angry, and sometimes abusive, even when the child is only a crying infant. Others find any social stimulation from their babies (whether smiling or crying) to be much more irritating than normal mothers do. Their abuse in turn adds to their anxiety and feelings of helplessness. If the woman is a second-generation or later generation out-of-wedlock mother, or if she is a teenager, she is less likely to know what the appropriate expectations of a young child should be. . . .

The most likely causes of child abuse by a mother, in fact, can be traced to the violence and substance abuse present in the mother's childhood, followed by the stress and discord in her current household. This is capped by her own victimization, and leads to increased illness and a hypersensitivity to the annoyances that children cause. In the period between her early experience with abusing parents and her later experiences with an abusing "mate," the future abusing mother frequently becomes more aggressive and deviant, developing a hostile and rebellious way of acting. She will associate more with men of similar hostility and eventually will "marry" them, becoming an abused spouse herself.

Considering this type of family background, it is no wonder that abusing families and mothers often are the most isolated. Increasingly, this isolation is most evident in the poorest neighborhoods in the United States. According to a National Incidence Studies survey, these communities have the highest incidence of serious abuse.

Children are at risk of being abused if they are in families in which they see abuse. Thus, child abuse often is linked closely to abuse of the mother. Significantly, in one study, 90 percent of women residing in shelters for battered women and children said their children were in the same room or the next room while they were being abused. This is telling because abused mothers were eight times more likely to hurt their children when they were being battered than when they were safe from their violent partners.

Tragically, changes in community moral norms over the past five decades are reflected in the profile of the child-killing mother. As compared with her counterpart 50 years ago, the mother who kills her children today is younger, has more children, and exhibits less of a conscience. In addition, many of her children are born out of wedlock. The next generation of child abusers is being formed in this environment; many will never know that children can be treated differently. . . .

A RETURN TO MARRIAGE

Fundamental changes are needed to correct the social drift toward family and community disintegration in the United States. Unfortunately, the well-intentioned efforts of the past three decades have not stemmed the tide. But they have done one thing: They have shown that the changes that must be made are beyond the capacity of government.

Many of these fundamental changes must take place within the most basic of institutions: the family unit. They must be supported by changes in local communities and reinforced by community institutions like the churches and their ancillary organizations that help the needy, as well as by programs like Big Brothers and Big Sisters. These institutions and organizations can have the greatest effect in reestablishing the centrality of marriage and promoting the married family unit as the best environment for the raising of America's children.

If the safest place for children is with their married biological parents, it follows that supporting marriage should be the foremost policy goal of every group concerned with the well-being of children. Local leaders, including members of the clergy and charitable organizations, can direct those who exhibit the characteristics of potential child abusers into intense marriage preparation programs to learn the skills and attitudes needed before they get married or start a family. Religious leaders play a vital role in strengthening the status of marriage and the family in communities of abuse. Not only has involvement in weekly worship been associated with the enduring intactness of marriage, but church affiliation in general has offered families a community of support. These two conditions have been shown to reduce significantly the incidence of child abuse.

THE DANGERS OF ILLEGITIMACY AND DIVORCE

Child abuse and neglect must be added to the long list of grave risks that out-of-wedlock birth and divorce place on the development of America's youth. In myriad ways (such as physical and mental health, cognitive and work abilities, addiction, crime, economic dependency, and unexpected pregnancy), illegitimacy weakens and warps significant numbers of children. Adult irresponsibility and lack of commitment in matters of sex, love, and marriage result in massive suffering for America's children. A Heritage Foundation study of the real root causes of violent juvenile crime illuminates how Americans are losing one of their most basic freedoms: the freedom to live and walk around safely in their own communities. Child abuse, after robbing children of a happy childhood, is contributing to the growing numbers of violent young people who diminish these freedoms.

Fatal abuse, serious abuse, and neglect are lowest in households with married biological parents, and highest in households in which the biological mother cohabits with someone who is not the parent. Cohabitation seems to be the biggest culprit in fostering the subculture of child abuse. That children whose parents are not married would be more at risk, aggressive, depressed, and disturbed is exactly what common sense would predict when parents refuse to build the small communities of love and nurturing called married families. If American society continues to give equal standing to married family life, single-parent family life, and cohabitation, it must expect continued high levels of child abuse. The future looks dismal for the children unless intellectual and cultural leaders recover their respect for the traditional institution of marriage and their courage to defend and promote it. Until that day, the profound love and commitment of adults to raise and nurture their offspring together will continue to decline, and children will continue to suffer.

The prognosis is bleak for the United States. The underlying demographic drift in family structure indicates the continuing breakdown of the American family, which can lead only to a continuing rise in child abuse. Until there is a turnaround in the number of out-of-wedlock births and a downturn in divorces, the United States will continue to build a culture of rejection. Nothing other than the fundamental reform of family life and sexual mores can promise a significant change for the better.

"Spanking and other legal forms of corporal punishment of children are some of the major causes of physical abuse."

CORPORAL PUNISHMENT CAN LEAD TO CHILD ABUSE

Murray A. Straus and Carrie L. Yodanis

Murray A. Straus and Carrie L. Yodanis contend in the following viewpoint that the practice of corporal punishment, more commonly known as spanking, often escalates into child abuse. Moreover, claim the authors, studies demonstrate that children who are physically disciplined are at greater risk of becoming abusive parents. The problem of child abuse cannot be solved, they maintain, until the link between corporal punishment and child abuse is recognized and addressed. Straus is the author of the book *Beating the Devil out of Them: Corporal Punishment in American Families*. Yodanis coauthored the chapter of *Beating the Devil out of Them: Corporal Punishment in American Families* from which this viewpoint is taken.

As you read, consider the following questions:

1. According to the authors, what leads abusive parents to increase the severity of physical punishments?
2. What three reasons do Straus and Yodanis provide to explain why corporal punishment has been ignored as a cause of child abuse?
3. What theories do the authors offer to explain the link between corporal punishment and child abuse?

> Ricky LeTourneau "was disciplined to death" by foster mother Deborah Wolfenden after she lost control of her temper and beat him in January 1990. . . . [She] lost the battle for control. She lost control of herself. She lost control over her temper and her ability to discipline reasonably.
>
> (*The Times Record*, Brunswick, Maine, April 27, 1992, p. 1)

Ricky's death illustrates the tendency for physical discipline to become physical abuse. There is a fine line between physical abuse and legal, socially approved spanking and other modes of disciplining children. A number of leading researchers argue that spanking and other legal forms of corporal punishment of children are some of the major causes of physical abuse. Despite this, the idea that spanking increases the risk that a parent will go too far and cross the line to physical abuse has been largely ignored. Corporal punishment is not mentioned as a possible cause of physical abuse in the many publications of the National Center on Child Abuse and Neglect or in 1993 reports of the U.S. Advisory Board on Child Abuse and Neglect. The U.S. Advisory Board on Child Abuse recommended that federal funds be denied to *organizations* that permit corporal punishment of children, and the National Committee to Prevent Child Abuse and Neglect (a major national voluntary organization) mounted a campaign against corporal punishment *by teachers*. Neither organization has said that *parents* should never hit children. . . .

THE RESEARCH EVIDENCE

Perhaps corporal punishment is absent from books and articles on preventing physical abuse because the research evidence is not convincing. Let's look at that evidence.

Margaret A. Lynch and Jacqueline Roberts studied 33 physically abusive families and found that corporal punishment was the most commonly used means of punishment, with 72 percent of the families frequently hitting their children. But since they did not have a comparison group of non-abusive parents, there is no way of knowing if the abusive parents used more corporal punishment than other parents.

Other studies however, did use comparison groups and found that abusive parents tend to use corporal punishment more than non-abusive parents. Selwyn M. Smith compared 214 abusive and 76 non-abusive parents and found that 50 percent of abusive mothers and 37 percent of abusive fathers frequently used corporal punishment on their children, compared to 13 percent of the non-abusive mothers and 10 percent of the non-abusive fathers. Similarly, R. Kim Oates compared 56 abusive and 56 non-abusive parents and found that 54 percent of abusive mothers frequently used corporal punishment versus only 11 percent of the non-abusive mothers.

Not all studies have supported the idea that abusive parents use corporal punishment more than non-abusive parents. Elizabeth Elmer compared 11 abusive and 12 non-abusive families and concluded that whipping and spanking were the most frequent forms of discipline in both the abusive and non-abusive families. Edwina Baher et al. found that of 25 abusive mothers, 12 used corporal punishment, which is probably less than the general population rate. Penelope K. Trickett and Leon Kuczynski compared 20 abusive and 20 non-abusive families and found that corporal punishment was the main form of discipline used by both abusive and non-abusive parents. They found, though, that 40 percent of abusive parents, but no non-abusive parents, used severe forms of corporal punishment, such as striking the child with an object or in the face, pulling hair, or spanking the child with pants down.

This approach is based on the escalation theory [the idea that spanking escalates into more serious physical violence], but tests it indirectly. It assumes that the more parents were themselves hit as children, the more likely they are to be heavy users of corporal punishment on their own children, increasing the risk that it will escalate into physical abuse. Three studies by Murray A. Straus and his colleagues have taken this approach. Straus studied the parents in the first National Family Violence Survey. David W. Moore and Straus studied a sample of 958 New Hampshire parents, while Straus and Christine Smith studied the Hispanic-American parents in the second National Family Violence Survey. All three studies found that the more the parents themselves were corporally punished as adolescents, the greater the percentage who went beyond ordinary corporal punishment with their own children and engaged in attacks severe enough to be classified as physical abuse. However, none of these studies used enough statistical controls for characteristics that overlap with corporal punishment and might be the "real cause" of the physical abuse.

ABUSE BEGINS AS DISCIPLINE

Clinical work with abusive parents has shown that much physical abuse starts as an attempt to correct and control through corporal punishment. When the child does not comply or, in the case of older children, hits back and curses the parent, the resulting frustration and rage leads some parents to increase the severity of the physical attack and kick, punch, or hit with an object. Ruth S. Kempe and C. Henry Kempe, for example, say:

> [Abusive parents] . . . may be discouraged when spanking obviously brings no result, but they truly see no alternative and grow depressed both by their own behavior and their babies' responses. Helplessly, they continue in the same vicious circle: punishment, deteriorating relationship, frustration, and further punishment.

David A. Wolfe et al. call this sequence "child-precipitated" abuse because it begins when a child misbehaves. If corporal punishment is not effective, abusive parents increase the severity of the punishment until the point where a child may be injured. Anne Devenson and Marian Marion reached similar conclusions on the basis of clinical evidence. Marion also points out that corporal punishment creates a false sense of successful discipline because of the temporary end it puts to undesirable behavior. She also cites research that shows the corporal punishment tends to *increase* undesirable behavior in children. So, parents who rely on hitting to control the child's behavior have to continually increase the intensity. Besides the clinically based conclusions we just mentioned, there has been some research on this increasing intensity, or escalation. Neil Frude and Alison Gross studied 111 mothers and found that 40 percent were worried that they could possibly hurt their children. These tended to be the mothers who used corporal punishment frequently. David G. Gil studied 1,380 abused children and found that 63 percent of the abuse incidents were an "immediate or delayed response to specific [misbehavior] of the child."

THE THEORY OF ESCALATION

The research by Alfred Kadushin and Judith A. Martin on 66 abusive parents is probably the most direct test of the escalation theory. They describe a number of specific situations in which escalation occurs such as a child who fails to respond to the punishment, attempts to fight back or run away, or the parent who becomes frustrated and then enraged when using corporal punishment, as in the following two examples:

> Then I started to spank her and she wouldn't cry—stubborn, she's just like I am, she wouldn't cry—like it was having no effect, like she was defying me. So I spanked her all the harder.

> It all started when Camille [age 14] slammed the door on her little sister's leg. Camille was in the bathroom and realized there was no toilet tissue. She asked her little sister, the 9 year old, to get some tissue, which she did do, and apparently her sister wasn't rushing out of the bathroom fast enough and Camille

kind of pushed the door, and in the process, she caught her sister's leg in the door, and with the child screaming as she did from the pain, it got me very angered. . . . And I think at that moment I lost control completely, and I went over and I swatted Camille with my—you know, my hand, and Camille turned around and she swung back to strike me, which she did do and that got me even more aggravated. And before I know what really was going on, I had pounded Camille several times. She had run a tub of bath water to take a bath, and suddenly I realized I had knocked Camille into the bathtub. And apparently I had struck her in the face, which by no means was intentional. But she had a swollen eye, and she didn't say anything to me that night.

EVALUATING THE EVIDENCE

Three of the five studies that compared abusive and non-abusive parents found that abusing parents were more prone to use corporal punishment or severe corporal punishment. Three out of five studies is far from conclusive. On the other hand, the clinical evidence, the indirect tests of the escalation theory by Straus et al. and the only scientific study, researched by Kadushin and Martin, that directly tested the idea that corporal punishment tends to escalate into physical abuse strongly supported the findings of the three studies.

A hard-nosed evaluation would point out that there has not been a definitive experimental study showing that corporal punishment causes physical abuse. On the other hand, that also can be said about every other presumed cause. The research evidence on corporal punishment is as strong or stronger than the evidence on other causes of physical abuse that have been studied, such as poverty or teenaged motherhood. Yet I have never heard or read a demand for definitive experimental evidence before teenaged motherhood or poverty can be considered causes of abuse.

At a 1993 conference to plan a national agenda on reducing family violence, many causes of family violence and how to prevent them were discussed. When I brought up corporal punishment, there was an instant demand for me to cite the evidence—something that had not been requested in the previous day and a half of the conference during which many potential causes of family violence were mentioned. I then outlined the evidence just presented and also the results of the research in this viewpoint. The rejoinder essentially was, It's all correlational evidence, and We need evidence based on randomized field trials. I agreed, but then pointed out that *none* of the strategies for preventing child abuse mentioned in the previous day and a half had been tested by a randomized trial experiment, yet no one objected.

Those who demanded experimental evidence on whether reducing corporal punishment will reduce the rate of physical abuse were correct. Their error was in not demanding the same level of evidence for other presumed causes of physical abuse.

Since the evidence on corporal punishment is as good (or no worse) than the evidence on other presumed causes of physical abuse, why the lack of attention to corporal punishment in books and literature on child abuse when a few respected scholars have concluded that spanking children is a major cause of physical abuse? We will consider three possibilities.

SPANKING IS ACCEPTED BY SOCIETY

Probably the main reason for ignoring the idea that corporal punishment is one of the causes of physical abuse is because the concept conflicts with cultural norms supporting corporal punishment. These norms influence social scientists, child-abuse professionals, parent educators, and parents. Almost everyone is against teenagers having children regardless of whether it is a cause of child abuse, so there is consensus that reducing teen-aged pregnancy would be a good way to reduce physical abuse and other social problems, such as welfare dependency. Corporal punishment, however, is something that 84 percent of the population thinks is necessary. So, both the general public and social scientists demand definitive evidence before concluding that corporal punishment is one of the causes of child abuse. At the national conference mentioned earlier, many potential causes were discussed. The only cause of physical abuse about which questions were raised because of lack of experimental evidence was corporal punishment. There seems to be a double standard concerning the evidence that is needed, and this leads many social scientists and almost all agencies concerned with preventing or treating physical abuse to dismiss corporal punishment. The same applies to agencies that fund research, and that reduces the chances of more definitive research being done.

There are many indicators of the degree to which corporal punishment is a culturally expected aspect of parent behavior:

- Corporal punishment is legal in every state of the U.S.
- At least 84 percent of Americans believe that "a good hard spanking is sometimes necessary," according to research conducted by Betsy A. Lehman.
- More than 90 percent of American parents use corporal punishment on toddlers, and more than half continue this into the early teen years.
- The laws permitting corporal punishment are not forgotten

features of an earlier period. The child-abuse legislation passed in all 50 states of the U.S. in the 1960s reconfirmed them by explicitly excluding use of corporal punishment from what is prohibited. Ironically, if the theory is correct that corporal punishment increases the risk of physical abuse, this legislation may have put children at *increased* risk of physical abuse by legally reinforcing the traditional appropriateness of corporal punishment.

- A study by Barbara A. Carson found that non-spanking parents tend to be perceived as ineffective and their children as badly behaved. Their neighbors, friends, and relatives offer indirect and sometimes direct suggestions to spank, such as, "What that child needs is a good spanking."

PERCEPTION OF PHYSICAL ABUSE IS DISTORTED

Another reason corporal punishment may be ignored as a cause of physical abuse is a distorted perception of physical abuse. This perception comes from the fact that newspapers and television—to attract more readers or viewers—tend to show only cases involving sadistic and mentally ill parents who burn, maim, and kill children. By contrast, 95 percent of physical-abuse cases do not involve severe injuries and typically are rooted in corporal punishment rather than psychopathology. This matches the conclusion reached by pioneer child-abuse researchers such as Richard J. Gelles, and Kempe and Kempe, who argued that psychopathology is involved in no more than 10 percent of physical-abuse cases. It is possible that the horrifying image of extreme but not typical cases diverts attention from the typical case, which is most often rooted in corporal punishment.

WHY THEORIES ON CORPORAL PUNISHMENT LEAD TO ABUSE

Still another reason books and agencies concerned with child abuse would ignore corporal punishment might be if there were no satisfactory explanations of how or why corporal punishment leads to physical abuse. Without an explanation, people tend to think the idea is preposterous. But there are, in fact, numerous theories about the link between corporal punishment and child abuse. Every author who has written about corporal punishment as a cause of physical abuse has offered an explanation. We have already considered one of these theories—the idea that much physical abuse occurs when parents escalate the level of the attack when their children continue to misbehave or strike back at them. The following section reviews three additional theories.

The idea behind the cultural spillover theory is that cultural norms that make violence legitimate for socially approved purposes, such as corporal punishment of children or capital punishment of murderers, tend to be applied to non-legitimate purposes, such as use of physical force and violence to obtain sex, namely, rape.

The results of a study of 958 New Hampshire parents are consistent with the cultural spillover theory because they show that parents who approved of corporal punishment had a much higher rate of going beyond that and severely assaulting their children than did parents who did not approve of corporal punishment. However, a study of 171 abusive parents by Deborah Shapiro did not support cultural spillover theory because a majority of the parents did not believe that spanking is the best form of discipline.

VIOLENCE BEGINS EARLY

Subabusive violence [corporal punishment] against children starts early—when an infant is still in nappies, in his cot at home, or at the kindergarten. Then it develops with the toddler, usually taking on stronger and more imposing forms, according to the child's age. Finally, in its school years and early adulthood aggression may become less obvious and adults may rely on more subtle or more hidden forms of violence. It is not suggesting that the violence becomes less abusive, but just less obvious. . . .

The majority of the adult population is convinced that the old, proven method of using subabusive violence against children is the right way to bring up their offspring. Therefore, they use and abuse the violence quite regularly and for almost any reason, explaining their brutality as a consequence of their love. Parents and teachers declare with conviction that they use violence against children out of love and care and for their own good.

Anna Piekarska, Journal of Interpersonal Violence, December 1996.

Another theory that might explain the link between corporal punishment and physical abuse involves depression. The more corporal punishment a person experienced as an adolescent, the greater the chance of being depressed as an adult. At first this may seem to contradict the long tradition of conceptualizing depression and suicide as internally directed aggression, with some people directing aggression inward and others outward in hostile acts towards others. But recent research shows that many depressed people do both. So, depression could be a link between having been a victim of corporal punishment and physically abusing a child.

The third theory was suggested by research showing that the more corporal punishment experienced as a child, the greater the chance of physically assaulting a spouse later in life. Putting this together with research showing that marital violence greatly increases the chance of physical abuse suggests that violence between the parents is the link between corporal punishment and physical abuse of children. . . .

How Corporal Punishment Leads to Abuse

During the past 25 years, many well-respected scholars have argued that corporal punishment by parents increases the chances that they will go too far and physically abuse their children. The scientific evidence showing that corporal punishment is a risk factor for physical abuse, although not conclusive, is as good or better than the evidence for other suspected causes. Despite the evidence and the prestigious backing of this theory, corporal punishment has been virtually ignored as a cause of physical abuse by government and private agencies, and by authors of books on child abuse.

The main reason corporal punishment is neglected is probably because hitting children to correct and control them is so deeply ingrained in American culture that the idea of eliminating it is regarded as ridiculous, outrageous, or impractical. One purpose of this viewpoint was to make that idea seem less ridiculous by setting forth a possible theory and testing that theory.

Our review of previous studies and our analysis suggest that corporal punishment can lead to physical abuse by a process that works at several levels. At the *immediate incident* level, escalation occurs in a specific sequence between a parent and child: a parent spanks a child, the child rebels rather than complies, and the now even-angrier parent attacks the child in a way that crosses the boundary between legal corporal punishment and physical abuse.

Viewed *developmentally*, the more corporal punishment is used, the greater the risk of escalation because corporal punishment does not help a child develop an internalized conscience and leads to more physically aggressive behavior by the child. So the more parents rely on hitting, the more they will have to do it over time, and the greater the chance of the child hitting back, further increasing the risk that corporal punishment will lead to physical abuse.

At the *macro-cultural* level, corporal punishment creates a social climate that approves of violence to correct wrongdoing and to achieve other socially desirable ends. This makes the public, and parents themselves, more tolerant of physical abuse. Cultural approval or tolerance of this sort is illustrated by a 1993 New Hampshire Supreme Court decision, which said that a child had not been physically abused even though he had welts visible five days after being beaten with a belt by his mother.

At the *inter-generational* level of analysis, corporal punishment increases the chance that when the child is an adult he or she will approve of interpersonal violence, be in a violent marriage, and be depressed. Thus, corporal punishment is one way physical abuse is transmitted from generation to generation.

INTER-GENERATIONAL ABUSE

Looking at subjects who answered a poll on corporal punishment, we found that more than half of the parents remembered being hit one or more times during their early teens, and that the parents who experienced corporal punishment were more likely to physically abuse their own children. Even one instance of being hit by parents at that age increased the chances of later being physically abusive. Parents who were hit the most had the greatest chance of physically abusing their own child.

Why does being hit as a child increase the chances of physically abusing your own children? We found three reasons: corporal punishment is tied in with attitudes favoring violence, with an increased chance of violence between the parents, and with an increased chance of depression. Each of these three reasons is associated with physical abuse. . . .

At the very least, our research suggests that more progress toward preventing physical abuse can be made if researchers and organizations concerned with reducing physical abuse stop ignoring corporal punishment. There is a certain irony in this conclusion because it is doubtful that any of the agencies mentioned in the introduction approve of parents hitting a teenaged child, yet they are silent on the issue. To start with, there should be programs to alert parents of teenagers to the risks they unknowingly subject their children to by hitting them even once. In the long run, we believe future research will show that this same principle applies to children of all ages.

"Children are far more likely to be
deprived of their basic needs by
parents who are depressed . . . than
by parents who are depraved."

DEPRESSION CAN CAUSE PARENTS TO ABUSE THEIR CHILDREN

Richard Weissbourd

In the following viewpoint, Richard Weissbourd maintains that feelings of depression can cause parents to abuse their children, especially when those feelings are exacerbated by life stresses and poverty. He claims that parental depression can lead to a wide range of abuse, from emotional neglect to severe physical harm. Weissbourd is the author of the book *The Vulnerable Child: What Really Hurts America's Children and What We Can Do About It*, from which this viewpoint is excerpted.

As you read, consider the following questions:

1. According to Weissbourd, how do the media portray abusive families?
2. In the author's opinion, how do children play destructive roles in relieving their parents' depression?
3. What areas of children's lives are affected by parents' depression, in the words of Weissbourd?

Reprinted from Richard Weissbourd, *The Vulnerable Child*, (pages 71–76), ©1996 by Richard Weissbourd, by permission of Addison Wesley Longman.

Why do so many children experience problems that are clearly rooted in their families? The answer to this question . . . lies in the qualities of parenting and in sibling relationships and family patterns. . . . An understanding of these aspects of families needs to guide the efforts of policy makers and professionals to strengthen children.

A LACK OF VALUES?

Many Americans, of course, blame the plight of children today on parents who lack values, who have abdicated some fundamental sense of responsibility for their children—or who have entirely lost their moral bearings. These images have been fed almost daily through the 1980s and 1990s by newspapers and talk shows that grimly parade stories of children brutalized by their parents; children chained to bannisters, stuffed into garbage cans, even immolated by their parents. In 1994, Speaker of the House Newt Gingrich, prompted by the story of Susan Smith—the mother who drowned her two sons and then pleaded publicly for help in finding them—promised to attack the "sickness" in American families. Some of these stories describe middle- and upper-class parents, including suburban parents who leave their children home alone and all-American families in which sexual abuse is rampant ("Unspoken Traditional Family Values: Abuse, Alcoholism, Incest," reads a Vermont bumper sticker). A proliferating self-help literature and at-risk family industry also trumpets the notion that self-indulgent middle-class parents have blighted their children's development, leaving children as adults, as best-selling author John Bradshaw puts it, with a "wounded, neglected child within." (Without a hint of irony or self-consciousness, two specialists in the at-risk family industry declared that 96 percent of American families are dysfunctional.) Yet the bulk of these stories describe poor parents, especially poor, crack-addicted mothers who visit horrors on their children. A small but growing number of Americans now clamor to solve this problem of depravity by removing children from their homes, by yanking them out of these moral swamps.

These images depict some families. Some parents appear to have lost some basic moral sense. Parents who sexually abuse their children have surely lost their moral compass. Workers who investigate neglect and abuse cases can reel off chilling accounts of very immature, narcissistic parents whose gross self-indulgence jeopardizes their children, such as parents who, wanting to party downstairs, lock their toddlers in an upstairs room. Teaching parents about their moral responsibilities and helping parents learn how to transmit important values to their children surely has to be part of our nation's efforts to strengthen children.

MISGUIDED MEDIA IMAGES

But these images distort and misguide on several counts. Most forms of neglect and abuse do not appear to be more prevalent today than they were in previous eras; some forms of neglect and abuse were far more widespread in other times. Child labor laws passed in the 1920s, for example, redressed a pervasive form of child maltreatment.

Most important, these images obscure a wide range of problems undermining parents that have little to do with defects or morality. If we are concerned about creating healthy conditions in which all children can grow, we need to find ways to help parents who suffer chronic stress and depression. Children are far more likely to be deprived of their basic needs by parents who are depressed, who feel helpless and hopeless, than by parents who are depraved. Similarly, although media attention has focused on the destruction caused by single parenthood, whether a primary caretaker is seriously depressed is more important to children than whether two parents live in a home. Behind every case of neglect and physical abuse there is a complex story, but it is stress and depression, not depravity or single parenthood per se, that typically play prominent roles. Moreover, when parents are depressed, children can be deprived of basic needs in subtle ways that do not constitute serious neglect or abuse. Poor parents in particular are more likely to experience not only hopelessness and the humiliation of unemployment and welfare dependency, but also health problems, mental illness, accidents, the death of family members or friends, hunger, eviction, among other difficulties, that create grinding anxieties and miseries that undercut their ability to meet their children's basic needs—and that sometimes lead to serious neglect and abuse.

PARENTS AFFLICTED BY DEPRESSION

Depression affects a staggering number of parents in the United States. Young children depend heavily on their mothers, and 12 percent of mothers of young children are depressed according to strict diagnostic criteria, and 52 percent report depressive symptoms. These parents are far less able than others to provide their children with almost all the ingredients of growth. Research shows that depressed mothers are less able to enter into the world of their infants and to be the physical, warm, encouraging, "I'm behind you, I'm with you, I'm here for you" presences that infants need. They have more difficulty mirroring their infants' facial gestures, and they tend to be less vocal and proximal (they play at a distance).

In addition to suffering from their parents' unresponsiveness, children of all ages sometimes play destructive roles in relieving their parents' misery. Sheila, a Boston parent, admits that before entering a family support program, when she started to feel helpless and overwhelmed she would hit and scream at her children because "they were the only things in my life I could control." A 16-year-old in Little Rock says that when her mother is depressed "she tries to drag me down with her." Bill, a parent in Baltimore, concedes that he looks to his eight-year-old daughter to buoy him, saddling her with what he knows is far too heavy a burden. Children faced with the mystery of a parent's depression may come to feel defeated and deficient. Diana, an eleven-year-old in Chicago, tells her therapist that she is worried that something is wrong with her because she can't cheer up her mother. Research shows that depressed parents also often resolve conflict with their children in ways that require little effort, either dropping initial demands at the first hint of resistance or issuing unilateral commands, and that measured, consistent forms of discipline tend to fly out the window. As child-development researcher Vonnie McCloyd writes: "Rewarding, explaining, consulting, and negotiating with the child require patience and concentration—qualities typically in short supply when parents feel harassed and overburdened."

THE LINK BETWEEN DEPRESSION AND CHILD ABUSE

Many areas of children's lives are affected by parents' depression. Because they are more likely to smoke, drink, and abuse drugs, including during pregnancy, depressed parents can be hazardous to their children's physical health. Maternal depression during pregnancy has been linked with low birth weight and with inconsolability in infancy. Behavior problems, somatic difficulties, learning problems, slow growth, emotional illness, even accidents are more likely to befall young children with depressed mothers. Failure to learn from parents effective strategies for dealing with stress and depression may also undermine children's friendships and romantic ties throughout childhood and adulthood and impair their own capacity to parent.

What makes this situation even more tragic is that depressed parents are likely to be keenly aware that their depression is sabotaging their parenting, understanding all too well that they are unreasonably impatient, for example. Yet given how dragged down and embattled they feel, they cannot do any better or stop their detrimental behavior.

Of course, parents do not need to lead consistently cheerful and frictionless lives to parent effectively. Children typically have little trouble rebounding when a parent suffers a temporary problem, such as an acute illness or an accident. Chronic, unrelenting stress or depression is another story, however. One study of unemployed fathers found that the likelihood of a father's describing his child negatively increased with the length of time he was unemployed. Children may be especially endangered when a parent who is frayed by long-standing problems must suddenly confront a crisis, such as the death of a family member or an unexpected financial burden. Abuse often occurs because an already depleted parent is pushed over the edge by yet another battle to be fought, another loss to be absorbed, another disappointment to be endured.

SOME CHARACTERISTICS OF ABUSIVE PARENTS

Abusive parents, when compared to nonabusers, show greater physiological reactivity, irritation, and annoyance in response to both their children's *positive and negative* statements and behaviors. They often perceive their own children as more aggressive, disobedient, stupid and annoying than other children, even though nonfamily observers see none of these problems in the children. Studies have identified parental characteristics associated with child abuse and neglect: low self-esteem, poor impulse control, depression, anxiety, and antisocial behavior including aggression and substance abuse.

The U.S. Advisory Board on Child Abuse and Neglect, *A Nation's Shame: Fatal Child Abuse and Neglect in the United States*, April 1995.

How badly children are hurt when a parent is depressed is, again, connected to many other, interacting circumstances. The child's temperament and coping abilities, the parent's coping strategies, whether the child is heavily dependent on the parent, how depression is explained to the child, whether the child is able to draw on the support of siblings, friends, or community adults, and whether families have resources to deal with crises all determine the extent and nature of the damage. Children in poor families often fare the worst not simply because poor parents suffer more crises, but because they have fewer means of coping with crises and releasing stress and typically have little time to recuperate. Research shows that crises in poor families' lives often come in rapid succession.

Parents cannot be protected from depression and other forms of mental illness that have a strong biological basis. Some parents also will suffer unrelenting stresses and hardships that plunge them into a depression that lasts many years. Yet the good news is that even when depression cannot be prevented or cured, parents can meet their children's basic needs. Research shows that knowledge should not be underestimated, that even when parents remain depressed they can learn parenting skills, such as effective disciplining methods, strategies for constructively expressing anger, and strategies for getting children to comply with requests, that keep their children on healthy developmental paths.

PREVENTING DEPRESSED PARENTS FROM BECOMING ABUSIVE

Basic knowledge about children and their development appears to be key in keeping depressed parents from becoming verbally or physically abusive. Research shows that abusing parents often greatly overestimate what children can do and attribute to babies hostile intent. For example, an abusing parent is more likely to think that a baby is crying because he or she is annoyed with the parent rather than because the baby is simply irritable. In one study, parents who received simply a newsletter instructing them about the developmental needs and tasks of infants and suggesting coping strategies were significantly less likely to hit their children than were parents who did not receive this newsletter. High-risk parents, including socially isolated parents and poor parents, were most likely to benefit.

Many sectors of our society need to be engaged in relieving stress on parents and in helping parents deal with depression. Employers who seek to reduce stress for parents, city governments that respond to parents' needs, parent and family support programs that help people support one another and that deal directly with stresses in parents' lives can all make a difference. Greater knowledge about which families are likely to suffer stress and depression, about the many ways in which children can be undercut by the troubles and limitations of their parents, about ways of preventing depression, and about parenting techniques that can allay the damage caused to children by parents' depression needs to be built into every layer of public policy—from how teachers and health-care workers tend to children and parents to how politicians think about large-scale public programs.

"Religious beliefs can foster, encourage, and justify abusive behavior."

RELIGION CAN FOSTER CHILD ABUSE

Bette L. Bottoms et al.

The authors of the following viewpoint allege that some religious beliefs promote behavior that is abusive toward children. According to Bette L. Bottoms and her colleagues, religiously justified abuse manifests itself in a variety of forms, including harsh physical discipline, attempts to exorcise children from "demonic spirits," and medical neglect by groups such as the Christian Scientists. Bottoms is a professor of psychology at the University of Illinois at Chicago.

As you read, consider the following questions:
1. How do some religious groups interpret the Bible as promoting the physical punishment of children, in the authors' opinion?
2. In the authors' view, how do certain religious groups justify the medical neglect of children?
3. According to Bottoms and her colleagues, what are some examples of churches' sanctioning or concealing child abuse?

Reprinted from Bette L. Bottoms, Phillip R. Shaver, Gail S. Goodman, and Jianjian Qin, "In the Name of God: A Profile of Religion-Related Child Abuse," *Journal of Social Issues*, Summer 1995, by permission of Blackwell Publishers and the authors.

In 1993, a California father was convicted of first-degree murder and sentenced to 25 years to life for drowning his 5-year-old daughter Lisa in a bathtub. His wife was convicted of second-degree murder. According to the Associated Press wire service, "Lisa's parents thought she was possessed by demons." They were attempting an exorcism. In 1978, David and Tammy Gilmore offered prayers to God, but sought no medical treatment, as they watched their 15-month-old son's flu-like symptoms slowly escalate from high fever to blindness, unresponsiveness, and finally, death. In 1993, Father David Holly, a Roman Catholic priest, was sentenced to 275 years for his admitted sexual molestation of eight young boys—probably only a subset of victims from a period of perpetration that had begun as early as 1968. In the late 1980s in Washington state, two adolescent sisters attended an emotional church-camp session on incest and then accused their father, Deputy Sheriff Paul Ingram, of incest and satanic cult abuse. Under the influence of his minister, the father learned to enter a trance state in which he (almost certainly incorrectly) "remembered" the satanic events.

These examples illustrate some of the ways in which religion is interwoven with allegations of child abuse in the United States. Religious beliefs can foster, encourage, and justify abusive behavior. The myriad connections between religion and child abuse led Donald Capps, a recent president of the Society for the Scientific Study of Religion, to entitle his presidential address "Religion and Child Abuse, Perfect Together." Although religious himself, Capps sorrowfully traced the indisputable connection between traditional religion and violence against children. Similar points were made in Philip Greven's chilling book, *Spare the Child: The Religious Roots of Punishment and the Psychological Impact of Physical Abuse.*

In the present viewpoint, we explore the complex role of religion in actual and alleged child abuse cases reported to us in the context of a nationwide survey of American mental health professionals. One objective of our survey was to determine the characteristics of child abuse cases that involve religion-related elements. To our knowledge, our sample of child abuse case reports involving religious beliefs is the largest ever to be examined quantitatively. We review the limited literature on the ways in which specific religious beliefs are involved in child abuse, then examine our own sample of cases. . . .

ORIGINS OF RELIGIOUSLY JUSTIFIED CHILD ABUSE
It may be hard for many Americans to believe that religiously justified child abuse occurs with any frequency. After all, reli-

gion is supposed to provide specific directives for moral action and the promotion of human welfare, not add to degradation and misery. Indeed, religious groups often play an active, positive role in prevention of child abuse and treatment of abuse victims. Yet, as historian Philip Greven points out, encouragement for violent, physically abusive child-rearing techniques can be traced to Biblical passages such as the following: "He that spareth his rod hateth his son: but he that loveth him chaseneth him betimes." "Withhold no correction from the child: for if thou beatest him with the rod, he shall not die. Thou shalt beat him with the rod, and shalt deliver his soul from hell" (Proverbs 13:24 and 23:13–14, respectively). Says Greven: "For believers in the literal reality of hell, salvation means escape and rescue from the eternity of suffering that many Christians believe awaits the bodies and souls of unsaved sinners. For many . . . hell is an actual, physical place of punishment, the locale of future suffering so vast, so extreme, and so permanent that our minds can hardly grasp the enormity of the threat."

In light of directives such as those from Proverbs, and belief in a vengeful God who would punish earthly pleasure with the ultimate torture of hell, both corporal punishment to enforce parental authority and actions designed to combat Satan make sense. It is thought that sin is the vehicle to hell, inspired by a literal Satan—ergo both sin and Satan must be stopped. Accordingly, it is better that children experience a temporary hell inflicted by loving parents than that they burn in an eternal hell.

Some believers extend a literal interpretation of religious writings so far as to equate children's misbehavior with the actual activity of Satan or other evil spirits who literally possess the children. Greven recounts an example: "She would fight at school until they whipped her and blood ran down her legs. 'The Devil's in her,' the teachers would tell her mother." Adults with such beliefs may consider it their duty to perform some kind of ritualistic exorcism to rid a child of evil. The outcome can be murderous—to the child's psyche, if not to the child's body. . . .

MEDICAL NEGLECT

Medical neglect dictated by religious beliefs is another route through which children become victims of religious ideology. Neglect, broadly defined, is the most common form of child maltreatment and can have severe consequences. Nevertheless, it receives little attention compared to sexual and physical abuse. Harm resulting from the deliberate withholding of medical care for religious reasons may be particularly serious because it is legally permitted in most jurisdictions, thus unlikely to be stopped. Perhaps because of this legal protection, religious motivations for child neglect have been largely ignored in the child abuse literature, even in work specifically examining medical neglect. Such avoidance of discussion and criticism of the negative effects of religion is in fact broadly characteristic of the medical and social sciences.

Religious groups most noted for shunning modern medicine include Jehovah's Witnesses, who do not believe in blood transfusions, and Christian Scientists, who favor prayer treatment over other medical procedures. In the *New England Journal of Medicine*, Christian Scientist Nathan Talbot stated that Christian Scientists are "caring and responsible people who love their children and want only the best possible care for them." But that "best possible care" includes treating children with prayer alone for such serious afflictions as leukemia, club feet, spinal meningitis, bone fracture, and diphtheria, all of which Talbot claims have been cured by prayer treatment alone. The mechanism for prayer curing? A practitioner, states R. Swan, whose "entire training . . . consists of two weeks of religious instruction" and whose services are often covered by insurance companies provides what N.A. Talbot calls "heartfelt yet disciplined prayer that brings to a case needing healing a deeper understanding of a person's actual spiritual being as the child of God. This understanding is held to be the crucial factor in dissolving the mental attitude from which all disease ultimately stems. . . . [Disease] is in the last analysis produced by a radically limited and distorted view of the true spiritual nature and capacities of men and women."

Other fundamentalist groups also believe medical treatment is a blasphemous intrusion into God's plan. For example, the religious ideology of Indiana-based Faith Assembly, as expounded by founder Hobart Freeman, is that "Satan controls the visible, sensory realm of nature, and he works through the occult forces of medicine, science, and education." Largely as a result of the members' avoidance of "satanic" modern medicine, during the late 1970s and early 1980s childbirth mortality in Freeman's group was 100 times greater for mothers and three times greater for their infants than rates in the general population.

WHEN CAN COURTS INTERVENE?

Such religious groups cite the First Amendment's prohibition of government interference with religion as legal justification for their negligence. Although other countries such as England and Canada legally mandate medical care for children, all but four of the United States (South Dakota, Hawaii, Massachusetts, and Maryland) grant some form of religious exemption to child protection. For example, in its definition of neglected and abused children, Virginia's statute excludes children who are "under treatment solely by spiritual means through prayer in accordance with the tenets and practices of a recognized church or religious organization."

In 1944 the Supreme Court ruled in the case of *Prince v. Massachusetts* that "the right to practice religion freely does not include liberty to expose the community or child to communicable disease or the latter to ill health or death." This directive was bolstered in 1982 by the Child Abuse Prevention and Treatment Act, which established states' responsibility to enforce newborn medical care. Even so, either because of their own personal beliefs, heavy lobbying from religious groups (particularly Christian Scientists), or reluctance to compromise First Amendment rights, state legislators have been steadfast in their scientifically unjustifiable position of retaining religious exemptions—supporting statutes that exempt parents and others from prosecution for harm to children resulting from religiously motivated medical neglect.

Even though courts can and often do intervene to order medical treatment for children at severe risk, because of legal exemptions religiously motivated child neglect is unlikely to be reported in the first place, even by professionals outside the church. To illustrate, a small survey study of medical doctors revealed that 71% would consider the parents' religious beliefs in their decision about whether or not to report medical neglect cases. When cases are reported, legal action against the perpetrators often stalls, even in the face of conclusive evidence. Worse yet, although religious exemptions are usually contained within child abuse and neglect statutes, they have also been used in defenses against more serious charges. For example, a California judge acquitted a Christian Science couple charged with manslaughter of their infant son who died of treatable bacterial meningitis. The judge decided that intermittent signs of improvement during the child's illness could be taken as evidence that prayer treatment did not necessarily constitute gross negligence. In so ruling, he applied a good-faith religious treatment exemption to manslaughter culpability.

Nevertheless, in the wake of several widely publicized child deaths and under pressure from various public and professional groups such as CHILD (Children's Healthcare is a Legal Duty) and the American Medical Association, exemption repeals are being sought in state legislatures, and legal sanctions against neglectful parents are being applied. For example, in perhaps the most publicized case of religiously motivated neglect, 2½-year-old Robyn Twitchell needlessly suffered the excruciating pain of an obstructed bowel for a week before he lapsed into a coma and died. Although Massachusetts maintained religious exemption laws at the time, a jury found parents David and Ginger guilty of negligent homicide. The Christian Science Church, according to A.A. Skolnick, considered the verdict a "gross intrusion of the First Amendment" and an "unmitigated attempt to undermine the Christian Science way of life." Ironically, although Christian Science ideology had allowed Robyn Twitchell only prayer treatment for his life-threatening illness, it had previously sanctioned his father's surgery for impacted wisdom teeth and his mother's anesthesia during his birth.

It may be a long while before legal exemptions for religiously motivated medical neglect are dismantled. Thus, such neglect is likely to continue. We thought it important to understand the nature of religiously motivated neglect cases, the harm done to victims, and the investigation and prosecution patterns associated with its disclosure.

ABUSE PERPETRATED BY RELIGIOUS AUTHORITY FIGURES

The news media have been flooded recently with claims of abuse perpetrated by religious officials, particularly Catholic priests. This abuse may be psychologically damaging for children who have been raised to fear God and revere the Church and its leaders. To child (and adult) parishioners, clergy are inherently powerful, trustworthy, and free by definition of mortal vice in much the same way as is God. This is illustrated in a recent comment by an attorney pursuing several child abuse suits against the Catholic Church: "We looked up to our teachers, to our Scout leaders, but not like we did to the priest. He was next to God." Child sexual abuse perpetrated by religious figures is often characterized by the same guilt, betrayal of trust, and shame common to familial incest. In the words of one victim, "The priest who's been approved by your parents is saying 'It's OK, this is normal.' I don't know if anyone can understand the guilt you feel at a moral level."

The Catholic Church's response has historically been to do nothing more than initiate surreptitious parish changes for offending priests. Only with the advent of recent media attention has the Church begun to investigate itself and admit the need for public accountability. Still, even writers in religiously oriented journals urge that suspicions of child abuse by religious leaders be reported to legal authorities rather than to ineffective Church officials.

Although speculations abound that Catholic celibacy requirements foster the tendency to sexually abuse children, sexual abuse is certainly not a problem confined to religious leaders of the Catholic faith. Our data include cases in which priests, ministers, and others with religious authority abused children. Although various incidence estimates have been advanced in media accounts, to date no one from the scientific community has systematically investigated the numbers of these cases being reported to therapists, the characteristics of these cases, and the psychological effects of this abuse on alleged victims. . . .

SUMMARY OF SURVEY RESULTS

We surveyed a national sample of over 19,000 clinical psychologists, psychiatrists, and social workers, and found that about one-third of the respondents had encountered cases of religion-related child abuse like those we described above: (a) abuse involving the withholding of medical care for religious reasons; (b) abuse related to attempts to rid a child of the devil or evil spirits; and (c) abuse perpetrated by religious professionals. Thus, religion-related abuse is not a rare phenomenon. Next, to obtain detailed information about cases, we conducted a follow-up survey of more than 2,000 of the professionals who had encountered a case. We conducted statistical comparisons of the three kinds of cases reported to us by the professionals. Next, we briefly summarize some of our findings.

First, we examined the types of maltreatment involved in the cases. Nearly all of the abuse perpetrated by religious professionals was sexual in nature. Apparently, the role of unquestioned moral leader has given religious authorities special access to children, similar to that of trusted family members in incest cases. About half of ridding-evil cases and a quarter of neglect cases also included allegations of sexual abuse. Physical abuse, psychological abuse, and neglect were present at different levels across the three types of cases. By definition, neglect characterized more withholding of medical care cases than other types of cases, but it was also noted in some cases of ridding a child of evil. Physical abuse occurred at a higher rate in ridding-evil cases than in other cases, and the physical abuse suffered by victims was often quite severe. For example, one respondent reported a case in which an "eyeball was plucked out of a youth's head during an exorcism ceremony." Psychological abuse was most commonly reported in child ridding-evil cases and adult medical neglect cases.

Second, we examined characteristics of the victims and perpetrators in the cases. Our data did not support the popular belief that most sexual abuse by religious authorities (particularly priests) is aimed at boys rather than girls and is perpetrated by men rather than women. Although more male than female perpetrators were reported, many females perpetrated such abuse. In addition, male and female victims were about equally common. Ridding-evil and neglect cases also were roughly equally divided between male and female perpetrators. Across all types of cases, the abuse was nearly always committed by people the children knew and trusted. In about half of the religious authority cases, the perpetrators were Catholic. Most ridding-evil cases involved fundamentalists or Protestants, and most neglect cases involved fundamentalists.

Finally, we investigated the psychological effects of religion-related abuse. Most victims initially sought therapy for depression. A striking proportion of those abused by religious professionals had even considered suicide. Severe dissociative disorders were seen in more than 20% of cases of ridding-evil and medical neglect.

DISCUSSION

In a 1988 review article, R.L. Gorsuch asked, "Is religion an important psychological variable?" When considering the abuse of children, our data [from our nationwide survey of mental health professionals] indicate that it is. We uncovered several factors that make religion-related abuse worth considering apart from other forms of child abuse. For example, religion-related abuse can be particularly damaging because young victims may come to believe the abuse is parentally or supernaturally sanctioned or required, or is a punishment for their own sins, as illustrated by these comments from different respondents:

> The older brother of a 10-year-old girl invoked religion in continuing sexual abuse that had been begun by another unknown adult. Victim was told it was God's punishment.

> Victim told mother when it happened. Mother told no one else and is still friendly with the offender-priest.

> Abuse was done by priest and his wife—the boys were told it was part of their religious obligation, they had to do it to be "good Christians."

> Victim had overt, chronic sexual abuse by both parents. She was

placed out of home with minister, who then fondled her because she was a "bad girl."

Religion-related abuse is particularly insidious when it is sanctioned or hidden by a church, causing victims to internalize blame and avoid disclosure, and, in turn, resulting in the perpetrators continuing their abuse as their chances for being discovered and punished are diminished. Our respondents noted organized church sanctioning of abuses:

> Grandmother reported she witnessed the child's abuse at church, justified by the religious idea of ridding children of the devil.

> Parents initiated request for a gathering of Pentecostal church members to pray together to rid 9-year-old girl of evil spirit. The mother felt powerless to control child. She joined charismatic church and out of desperation had child prayed for in front of church.

> Coverups by churches were also noted:

> In all five cases, the fact that the abuses were perpetrated by the clergy with the approval of the Catholic church made it difficult for the children to believe their feelings of being abused. . . . At first, they believed they were wrong or bad, not the church.

Such practices, perhaps most widely noted in the Catholic Church, led sociologist Andrew Greeley (himself a priest) to write in his preface to Jason Berry's book on sexual abuse by Catholic priests, "Bishops have with what seems like programmed consistency tried to hide, cover up, bribe, stonewall; often they have sent back into parishes men whom they knew to be a danger to the faithful. . . . Catholicism will survive, but that will be despite the present leadership and not because of them." Other religions may also be at fault for coverups. For example, one clinician wrote of a Jehovah's Witness congregation's response to her male client's charges of sexual abuse against their minister: "Victim aware that revealing sexual abuse by minister would likely (and did) result in 'disfellowship,' isolation from all significant others, due to his 'lie.'"

Of course, not all abuse is performed with a church's tacit permission, as illustrated in this example: "Father believed son was possessed by devil and that he must be stopped from influencing others. Father took son to Catholic priest to be exorcised. Priest called social services. . . ."

OTHER FORMS OF RELIGION-RELATED ABUSE

It is important to note that in this viewpoint, we have ignored other forms of religion-related child abuse that are of importance and need future examination if we are to fully understand the point at which religion fosters damaging abuse rather than compassionate child rearing. As an example, one of our clinicians wrote about the abuses reported by several adult clients who attended Catholic schools in their childhood: "They reported crowded classrooms with poorly trained, ill-equipped teachers who ruled by playing on the children's fear of hell and sin. It locks the children into self-doubt, fear of authority, impairment of adult identity."

Reprinted with permission of John Branch

Perhaps the most obvious of the forms of abuse we did not investigate is severe physical punishment for disciplinary reasons rooted in religious ideology. One of our respondents wrote, "In addition to these cases, I have seen several others (maybe two dozen) in which there was neglect and/or physical abuse and the parents related their actions to their religious value systems (i.e., 'spare the rod, spoil the child'), but I would not consider them to be abuse inspired by religion as much as abusive parenting rationalized by religion." We do not agree with this respondent's conclusion, nor would others such as Greven and Capps who have written about this form of religiously motivated and sanctioned abuse. Some nonmainstream religious groups and isolationalist cults have been found to practice severe beatings in the name of Godly discipline. When discovered, such cults' abusive practices and even their particular religious beliefs are immediately highlighted in the news media, and criticized and rejected by society with much self-righteousness. Yet how different are these beliefs and practices from those of many Methodist, Baptist, or Catholic parents? As Greven notes, abusive parenting styles have been driven by mainstream religious beliefs for centuries. They are part of our Euro-American heritage, and if religion-related child abuse is not acknowledged now as a problem by our society and its law-makers, it will be our legacy to the future.

Social scientists in general and child abuse researchers in particular have tended to steer clear of connections between religion and child abuse. There is little information about how religion relates to spending time with children, using various child-rearing techniques with children, allowing religious professionals to abuse children, and so on. We analyzed information made available by the windows of social service investigations and psychotherapy sessions; we have no way of moving from our data to base rates in the general population.

Finally, another type of religion-related abuse we have not discussed here, but we have studied, is abuse perpetrated in the name of Satan. Our research has led us to believe that "Satanic ritualistic abuse," as it has come to be called, is more of an unfounded panic than a real phenomenon. We found very little evidence for cases that have been reported to mental health professionals and legal authorities. In fact, one of our respondents, the head of a child and adolescent psychiatry unit at a prominent mental health center, commented: "The cases I report herein are sad: an adult recalling abuse by fundamentalist parents who may have been psychotic, two children who were abused by fundamentalist parents who believed that they were carrying out Biblical injunctions. These are bad enough situations without having the general population alarmed about some sort of satanic conspiracy." We agree. Our study leads us to believe there are more children actually being abused in the name of God than in the name of Satan. Ironically, while the public concerns itself with passing laws to punish satanic child abuse, laws remain established that protect parents whose particular variants of belief in God deny their children life-saving medical care. The freedom to choose religions and to practice them will, and should, always be protected by our constitution. The freedom to abuse children in the course of those practices ought to be curtailed. In the long run, society should find ways to protect children from religion-related abuse and to help religions evolve in the direction of better treatment of children.

> "Parents who are themselves deficient because of their own emotional deprivation are unable to offer empathy to their children."

MULTIPLE FACTORS CONTRIBUTE TO FATAL CHILD ABUSE

Susan Crimmins et al.

In the following viewpoint, Susan Crimmins and her coauthors contend that a high percentage of women convicted of murdering their children suffered emotional, physical, or sexual abuse in their own childhoods. The experience of child abuse, the authors maintain, renders some women incapable of the emotions and skills necessary to care for a child. Crimmins works as a clinical social worker with individuals who have experienced loss, trauma, and violence in their lives. She was the project director of the Female Drug Relationships in Murder (FEMDREIM) study, from which much of the data in this viewpoint originated.

As you read, consider the following questions:

1. What is the difference between a "mad" mother and a "bad" mother, according to the authors?
2. According to the authors, why are some people unable to develop positive and healthy attachments with others?
3. What percentage of the women in the FEMDREIM study suffered physical or sexual harm as children?

Reprinted from Susan Crimmins, Sandra Langley, Henry H. Brownstein, and Barry J. Spunt, "Convicted Women Who Have Killed Children," *Journal of Interpersonal Violence*, February 1997, vol. 12, no. 1, pages 49–69, by permission of Sage Publications, Inc.

The innocence and vulnerability of children, particularly of infants, typically arouse instincts of nurturance and protectiveness on a universal level. In addition, sociocultural expectations dictate that women are primary caretakers for the young. What then, would prompt a woman to kill an infant or child who is helpless and dependent upon her for survival?

Research shows that about two-thirds of the victims of women who commit homicide are family members, with the most common event being the killing of a spouse or partner. Research concerning women killing children is narrow in scope and often anecdotal in presentation due to small numbers. The paucity of reports on this topic may be related to truly low incidence of the crime, the underreporting or mistaken reporting of these crimes, or a combination of both. Crib deaths or Sudden Infant Death Syndrome (SIDS) overlap many times with the less socially acceptable report of infanticide. Another complicating factor is the number of missing children reported each year, which may mask a more accurate count of child deaths by mothers. However, we do know that homicide remains one of the top five leading causes of death during early childhood in the United States.

Despite the relative infrequency of reports of child killing by mothers, as compared to the overall homicide rate, its seriousness and moral implications render it worthy of further examination to identify contributing factors as well as to reflect upon society's handling of such violence. Data derived from interviews with women convicted of killing children are presented in an attempt to understand the factors that contribute to committing such an exceptional crime.

PERSPECTIVES ON THE MOTIVES FOR KILLING CHILDREN

Child killing has occurred throughout the ages, although the reasons given for its existence have varied. Malformation of the infant, economic distress, and social disgrace were all prevalent motives in dispensing with children, and killing was the most efficient method of ensuring that the burden was eliminated permanently. Additional literature has suggested that infant and child killing has also been influenced by complicating factors of jealousy and revenge, psychiatric conditions, and violence within families.

The 1922 Infanticide Act and, later, the Not Guilty by Reason of Insanity (NGRI) plea allowed the first opportunity to peer into the mind and intent of the mother who kills her child. These legal concepts also set the stage for controversy and labeling in attempting to decipher if these mothers were "mad or bad" in their killings. "Mad" mothers were believed to be psychiatrically unstable and killed as a result of their mental illness, whereas "bad" mothers were considered intrinsically evil and killed because of this predisposition.

Contemporary motives for killing children involve more psychological reasoning than having enough food to provide or being a victim of social disgrace. Revenge, sometimes referred to as the Medea Syndrome, involves the killing of children in an attempt to punish the husband or partner. Greek tragedy portrays Medea as the jealous, vengeful wife who gets back at her husband, Jason, by murdering their two children. Although this drama may be sensationally appealing, it leaves us with the question of why angry wives choose this pathological means of revenge toward their husbands when there are many other options available to them.

In recent literature, additional motives or reasons for these killings fall under the rubric of: acute psychosis or gross mental pathology; unwanted child; mercy killing; victim-precipitated; childhood maltreatment of women ("learned violence"); and poverty, stress, "social disorganization." R. Silverman and L. Kennedy distinguish between two different types of female child killers. The Type 1 mother commits infanticide due to severe psychological stress and is usually young, single, and immature. The Type 2 mother kills her child because she goes "too far" in physical abuse of the child, which may be the result of displaced anger, either conscious or unconscious. More often than not, she is married. The "goes too far" or Type 2 hypothesis is also proposed by P. Scott who theorizes that killing is the result of learning or frustration for these women. Perhaps A. Daniel and J. Kashani advance this thinking by linking the theory of intergenerational violence within families as the basis for the killing. They suggest that a mother with a history of physical abuse and serious psychopathology is a strong candidate for murdering a child. . . .

THE ROLE OF SELF-WORTH

How you feel about yourself is largely influenced by how others conveyed they felt about you during your youngest years. During early childhood, a mother is usually the person upon whom you can rely for security, warmth, and feelings of comfort. An absence of nurturance by a primary caretaker will interfere with the ability to develop positive feelings about yourself or the ability to build positive social experiences, unless alternative social and emotional supports are in place. Without having a "secure base" from which to operate, one is unable to develop positive or healthy attachments with others. In situations where the mother may be emotionally unavailable to her child (e.g., mental illness, neglect) and other supports are absent, the child grows up with an impoverished emotional repertoire from which to gauge interpersonal relationships and an adequate sense of self-worth. When this child grows up and becomes a mother, she is then unable to give her own child a sense of warmth or security, for as a "motherless mother," she cannot give what she has not been given.

There are several other areas of trauma that we know have deleterious effects upon the formation of personality or self in children who have early and prolonged exposure to them without the ameliorating benefits of social supports. Specifically, growing up in a family where alcohol and/or drugs are used on a regular basis or growing up where serious physical harm and sexual harm compromise a child's sense of safety and trust. Both of these scenarios are likely to result in the child developing a history of substance abuse to ward off feelings of psychic pain, as well as a plethora of mental health problems, including depression and suicidal behavior. . . .

What, then, are the experiences and sense of self held by women who kill children? Are they too damaged to care adequately for children? If so, what are the primary, damaging factors that so influenced their lives and development to the extent that they were rendered unable to care for and protect their children? Why did they resort to committing an act of lethal violence? These issues were examined via interviews with women who have been convicted of killing children.

THE FEMDREIM STUDY

This analysis is part of a study funded by the National Institute of Drug Abuse (NIDA) of women who have been convicted of murder or manslaughter in New York State. The purpose of the Female Drug Relationships in Murder (FEMDREIM) study was to examine the relationship between drugs and homicide committed by women within the state of New York. Four hundred and forty-three (443) women were identified by the New York State Department of Correctional Services (DOCS) as potential subjects in the study because they met one of two criteria:

1. Serving sentences in New York State prisons for murder or manslaughter between March 1992 and May 1993.
2. On active parole supervision in New York City as of spring 1993 for these crimes.

Our staff were not able to contact 143 of these women due to reasons such as: death, final stage illness, discharge from prison to upstate parole offices, or severe mental health disabilities. Of the remaining 300 women, 217 agreed to participate in the study, yielding a response rate of 72%. Two women gave incomplete information, resulting in 215 completed interviews. . . .

Official records indicate that 86 (or 19%) of the women identified as subjects were incarcerated for the death of a child. Of those, 42 women (49%) participated in an interview. Findings from these 42 interviews are the focus of this viewpoint. . . .

Examination of relevant interview data clearly indicates that many of these women were exposed to multiple experiences of damage that influenced their lives and their ability to parent children.

MOTHERLESS MOTHERS

Twenty-seven of the women (64%) were categorized as being motherless mothers based upon their reports of early experiences with their own mothers. Several types of behaviors resulted in the subjects' mothers being unavailable to them: serious and prolonged verbal abuse, serious physical abuse, alcoholism, mental health problems, and absence due to neglect/death. More than a third of the women (38%) had alcoholic mothers, 19% experienced serious physical abuse by their mothers, and the mothers of 17% were absent. Almost a quarter of the women (24%) had mothers who had more than one characteristic that made them unavailable to these subjects during childhood.

Alma spoke about the immediate effects that being abused had upon her:

> I didn't have a family life. My mother used to sit on my head to make me still so she could beat me with a cord, belt, or anything she could get her hands on, and things got worse when she burned me with an iron, and she allowed certain relatives to have sex with me and get away with it. She sexually abused me too. . . . [All the abuse] made me feel less important and didn't care about myself too much.

Later in the interview, Alma also spoke about how her childhood abuse affected her parenting skills with her 4-year-old son.

> I was very scared 'cause I was pregnant and I was scared. I didn't know what to do because my daughter's father left me alone 'cause he got me pregnant and I was ready to move. I was packing up my stuff and my son was acting up and I didn't know what to do 'cause I don't understand nothing about disciplining a child 'cause I was raised by my own family, how they abused

me and I didn't know what to do, so I took it out on my son and sent him to his room and I made him go to bed and he went to bed. I went near and he wasn't breathing, he stopped breathing, wouldn't breathe. I know he was sleeping and he didn't wake up. I hit him, I only hit him twice in the head with my hand. I don't know, with my shoe, my flat shoe in the head twice and that was it, and I sent him to his room 'cause I didn't want to hit him no more. . . . It was very hard for me 'cause I didn't know what to do. The only thing I knew was to take him to the doctor when he needed to go to the doctor and feed him and keep him clean, that was it. I didn't know how to love him, 'cause I didn't have, didn't love myself, I didn't know how to love him.

Slightly more than half (52%) of the women who killed children were motherless mothers who also had been involved with an abusive partner. A likely reason these women became involved with abusive partners was because their self-perceptions were damaged to the extent that they believed abuse was all they deserved. Only 12% of the women who were motherless mothers did not become involved with an abusive mate. An additional 26% were not characterized as motherless mothers but still became involved with an abusive partner. Although this group of women did not fit the description of being a motherless mother, they did have mothers who may be considered codependent in their behaviors. The possible impact this may have had upon the subjects' becoming involved with an abusive partner requires further research.

DRUG AND ALCOHOL ABUSE

Twenty-five of the 42 women (60%) reported that drugs/alcohol were used in their families of origin on a daily basis. Alcohol was overwhelmingly the most commonly used drug, as it was used on a daily basis in 24 of the families (57%). As previously mentioned, more than half of the 25 women were in families where the mother used alcohol on a regular basis. For these women, one can assume that their mothers were unavailable to them emotionally and were unable to provide them with the safety and comfort a child requires. Thus emotional abandonment was a common experience for these women, who, in turn, could not provide for their own children the safety and nurturance that they never had.

In terms of their own usage, 27 women, or 64%, of the group described using drugs or alcohol on at least a regular basis. *Regular basis* was defined as using 3 or more days per week for a month or more. The most common drugs that were used regularly by the 27 women were marijuana (11 or 26%), alcohol (8 or 19%), and tranquilizers (7 or 17%). Eighteen respondents, or 43%, who reported growing up in families where alcohol or drugs were used on a regular basis also reported regular alcohol or drug usage in their own lives. . . .

Sexual and Physical Harm

Three-fourths (74%) of the women said they witnessed or experienced serious physical and/or sexual harm during childhood. Two-thirds of the women witnessed or experienced serious physical harm, and half witnessed or experienced sexual harm. Most of the serious childhood physical harm was witnessed or experienced by the subjects equally with their mothers and with siblings (10 or 24%). On the other hand, most of the serious sexual harm during childhood was witnessed or experienced by the women with their father, stepfather or mother's boyfriend (9 or 21%), other relatives (i.e., male cousins, grandfathers), 8 or 19%, and then male siblings (6 or 14%). Thus an overwhelming majority of the harm witnessed or experienced by these women as children occurred in their own families among people they were supposed to trust or with whom they should have felt safe.

Thirty of 42 (71%) women reported that they had been victims of serious harm. All 13 of the women who experienced sexual harm were also victims of serious physical harm. Two-thirds of the women (67%) were physically harmed by husbands or boyfriends. Another 11 women, or slightly more than one-quarter of the sample (26%), reported that sexual harm toward them was committed by partners. Again, in relationships where a certain degree of intimacy and trust is expected, we see that these relationships are characterized by behavior that has rendered the woman unsafe.

The Case of Lisa

Lisa explained how the effects of being abused affected her self-esteem.

> When I was home from school one day and my mother had to go out for awhile, my older brother came in my room and forced me to have sex with him. I didn't want to, so he beat me up a little first and said he'd kill me if I told anyone. I can see now that I had very low self-esteem and would do anything for someone to love me.

Later in the interview, Lisa described how she ended up killing her own child to maintain the love of another and to preserve her own safety.

I had gotten up, taken a shower and gotten dressed. Then I was walking down the street to catch the bus, and I missed the bus by 2 seconds. I walked back home and got my mother up and asked her to take me to work. She got up, got dressed, and had a cup of coffee and drove me to work. We hardly ever even speak. She didn't speak to anybody that day. When I got to work I went to the bathroom, got my things out of my locker, then went up and counted out my drawer. It was early in the morning that day so it was difficult. It was back and forth to the bathroom. [You were pregnant?] Yes. I was basically a robot that day just going through the motions and not really feeling anything. I was having pains and I wanted to go home, but I couldn't tell anyone I was pregnant. I just couldn't. [What month were you?] Ninth. [You weren't showing?] I guess to some people I was, but I basically wear big shirts to begin with so nobody knew. They may have suspected, but they didn't really know. I wasn't allowed to tell anybody that I was pregnant because the child's father threatened to kill me and that person I told it to. I took his threat very seriously. . . . I went out to lunch and the pains got worse. Came back to work. I wanted to leave so bad but I couldn't 'cause I wouldn't get relieved till 5 o'clock. I kept on checking out the customers and the pain got worse and worse and worse. I just wanted to go home and tell my mother to take me to the doctor but I couldn't. I went back into the bathroom and as I was sitting on the toilet, something came out. I don't really know what happened from there. It's still a blur, but all I remember is that I took a box cutter and cut his throat. Then I stuffed some toilet paper in his mouth so he wouldn't make no noise. [What did you do with the body?] I put it in the trash.

SUICIDE ATTEMPTS

In addition to experiencing harm at the hands of others with whom there should have been trust, 17 of the 42 women (41%) reported that they also inflicted harm upon themselves. It is striking that of the 17 women who reported that they tried to kill themselves, most of them (14) tried to kill themselves more than once. These figures were not significantly different from the rest of the sample. Of the women convicted of killing a child, 59% reported a history of emotional or mental health problems, compared to 37% of the other women in our sample. The most common method of self-harm was overdose with various legal drugs (13 or 31%), followed by cutting wrists (6 or 14%). . . .

THE LINK TO LETHAL VIOLENCE

For the sample of women discussed herein, there was no single factor that led them into actions of lethal violence. Rather, their early years were characterized by various kinds of that were followed immediately by gross insensitivity to ̲r emotional needs. This was typically the result of inade-̲ ̲ate parenting and a paucity of social supports. Thus losses ̲evolved into traumas that eroded their sense of self, and when self no longer exists, the roots of violence are born. Blatant disregard of these women's childhood needs was so profound that their voices were silenced and their spirits broken at very early ages. These women, too, were betrayed by those who should have protected them. Their voices, even when exercised, were to no avail. The learned, maladaptive methods of coping with harm and trauma (e.g., drug and alcohol abuse), in turn, exacerbated the women's difficulties and left them vulnerable to becoming involved in additional situations of harm. Pervasive social isolation, coupled with their learned silence, only served to reinforce the cycle of poor self-esteem that had been initiated in their families of origin. Self was sacrificed in an attempt to remain connected to a larger social community called humanity. Factors that resulted in their resorting to lethal violence were built upon years of frustration, prior experiences of using violence as a means to "settle" disputes, and a desperate wish to alter their life situations, either immediately or long term.

A Loss of Control

Studies of the parenting adequacy of mothers sexually abused as children suggest reasons for perpetuation of the cycle [of abuse]. P.M. Cole et al. found that mothers who had experienced incest differed from comparison mothers "in feeling less confident and less emotionally controlled as parents." Compared to the control mothers, they reported more loss of control and less consistency with their children. Cole theorized that the loss of control and inconsistency might very likely promote such behavior in their children. An out-of-control mother paired with an out-of-control child is a dyad at high risk for maltreatment, particularly physical abuse.

Susan Zuravin et al., *Journal of Interpersonal Violence*, September 1996.

Periodic expressions of rage became assertions of vitality in an attempt to keep self alive. Deprivation, loss, and abuse so depleted the self that defending itself becomes of paramount importance. As A. Miller stated, "If their psyche is killed, they will learn how to kill—the only question is who will be killed: oneself, others, or both." H. Kohut said that empathy involves others making an effort to understand self. Parents who are themselves deficient because of their own emotional deprivation are unable to offer empathy to their children's developing sense of self. When emotional needs are consistently unmet, attachments to others are disrupted and self-esteem does not develop in a healthy way. If empathy is an extension of self, then the child who has a poor sense of self is unable to feel compassion for others. When "self-objects," such as parents, lack empathy, the child often develops an insecure sense of self as a result of feeling low self-worth, isolation, and rejection. Such feelings often generate additional feelings of rage and despair that later erupt into violent, aggressive behaviors.

A VICIOUS CYCLE OF ABUSE

Women who kill children are still somewhat of an enigma in the latter part of the 20th century. Whereas reasons and motives are complex, the literature still tends to focus upon these women as mad or bad. In an attempt to skirt further examination of this dichotomized thinking, attention has been diverted from the perpetrator and shifted onto the victims. Thus little is still known about those women who commit this crime. . . .

At the end of the interview, each woman was asked what type of advice or recommendations for programming she would give to women who found themselves in situations similar to her own. The emphasis of the women's suggestions points to rectifying those life situations and circumstances that have been outlined as self-damage indicators. Almost half (45%) of the women suggested that programs where their self-esteem could be developed were critical to their successful functioning. Low self-esteem, reliance upon a dysfunctional partner, and feelings of worthlessness characterized these women to the extent that their judgment about safety for themselves and their children was impaired. Due to the tremendous guilt feelings about their crime and to being ostracized within the prison system, as well as in society at large, these women hoped for a program that would help them deal with the loss of their children. Currently, there are no programs in prison for those who lost or killed a child. Women also wanted more parenting programs available to teach them about how to care for their children and to identify their children's needs. Programs addressing domestic violence were also important to these women, who stated that they first must learn to care for themselves before they could adequately care for their children.

Acknowledging and identifying women who are perpetual victims is possible via day care centers, school programs, and child health care systems. However, outreach and subsequent education to prevent violence is a major effort that requires interest, skill, empathy, and resources. The findings here support the aggressive use of prevention and intervention services regarding the identification of parental needs and fulfillment of those needs. Self-esteem builders and self-care programs for new mothers should also be offered in communities while providing nursery care for newborns. If we can correct the deficits of living in those who give life, we stand a chance of breaking the cycle of abuse and offer a future to children who otherwise may have been robbed of one.

PERIODICAL BIBLIOGRAPHY

The following articles have been selected to supplement the diverse views presented in this chapter. Addresses are provided for periodicals not indexed in the *Readers' Guide to Periodical Literature*, the *Alternative Press Index*, the *Social Sciences Index*, or the *Index to Legal Periodicals and Books*.

Cameron W. Barr	"Getting Adults to Think in New Ways," *Christian Science Monitor*, September 16, 1996.
Frank Bruni	"In an Age of Consent, Defining Abuse by Adults," *New York Times*, November 9, 1997.
Mary Eberstadt	"Pedophilia Chic," *Weekly Standard*, June 17, 1996. Available from 1211 Avenue of the Americas, New York, NY 10036.
Naamah M. Ford	"Broken Vows: A Hidden Abuser of Children," *Destiny*, April 1996. Available from 18398 Redwood Hwy., Selma, OR 97538.
Susan Gilbert	"Two Spanking Studies Indicate Parents Should Be Cautious," *New York Times*, August 20, 1997.
Edward Grimsley	"Keeping Children on the Straight and Narrow," *Conservative Chronicle*, February 14, 1996. Available from 9 Second St. NW, Hampton, IA 50441.
Nina George Hacker	"The 'Love' That Dares Not Speak Its Name," *Family Voice*, February 1996. Available from Concerned Women for America, 370 L'Enfant Promenade SW, Suite 800, Washington, DC 20024.
William R. Mattox Jr.	"Yes, You Can Spank Responsibly," *USA Today*, November 14, 1996.
Mindszenty Report	"Sex-Ploitation: Target Youth," October 1995. Available from PO Box 11321, St. Louis, MO 63105.
James Podgers	"When Does Punishment Go Too Far?: Courts Struggle to Find the Line Between Parental Discipline and Child Abuse," *ABA Journal*, October 1996.
Andrew Peyton Thomas	"Spanking the Anti-Spankers," *Weekly Standard*, September 8, 1997.

ARE FALSE ALLEGATIONS OF CHILD SEXUAL ABUSE A SERIOUS PROBLEM?

CHAPTER PREFACE

Since the early 1990s, a number of adults have accused their parents of sexually abusing them as children based on memories they claim to have repressed during childhood and only remembered as adults. Allegations such as these have initiated intense debate over whether incidents of traumatic child sexual abuse can be forgotten and then recollected years later.

The most vociferous critic of the validity of repressed memories is the False Memory Syndrome Foundation (FMSF), an organization that provides support to parents who have been accused of child sexual abuse based on repressed memories. FMSF members contend that such allegations occur as a result of misguided therapists' planting "false memories" in their patients through the use of manipulative techniques such as hypnosis. Critics assert that these techniques can be used to manipulate the mind into believing in things that never happened. Furthermore, those who reject the legitimacy of repressed memories argue that most repressed memory accusations verge on the ridiculous, with some "victims" claiming to remember being molested in their cribs.

On the other hand, many insist that repressed memories should be trusted. According to defenders of repressed memory theory, research demonstrates that the mind often responds to traumatic events by repressing painful memories; later in life, the recollection of abusive incidents may be triggered by a variety of events—including, but not limited to, therapy. In fact, proponents assert, many victims recall incidents of child sexual abuse without the aid of therapy. Furthermore, they maintain, even if therapists were intentionally manipulative, they would find it nearly impossible to create false memories of child sexual abuse. While human memory can be manipulated in some instances, supporters contend, therapists cannot introduce false memories of events as traumatic as child sexual abuse.

The lack of physical evidence in most recovered memory cases creates the difficult problem of determining the veracity of memory. This and other problems associated with the assessment of child sexual abuse accusations will be examined in the following chapter.

"When it comes to child abuse, the accused is guilty until he proves himself innocent."

THE CHILD PROTECTION SYSTEM PURSUES FALSE ALLEGATIONS OF CHILD SEXUAL ABUSE

Armin A. Brott

Armin A. Brott argues in the following viewpoint that the child protection system's overzealous pursuit of child sexual abusers has led to an alarming rise in false allegations. According to Brott, social workers seek to validate abuse claims instead of determining their veracity. In an attempt to conceal their coercive interviewing techniques, claims Brott, social workers often refuse to tape their interviews with children or destroy their notes after filing reports. Brott is a marketing consultant and writer in Berkeley, California.

As you read, consider the following questions:

1. According to Brott, what are some examples of the "incredibly broad powers" held by Child Protective Services?
2. In Brott's opinion, how might a doctor's report that an examination was "consistent with abuse" be misleading?
3. How do false allegations affect the wrongly accused, according to Brott?

Reprinted from Armin A. Brott, "A System Out of Control: The Epidemic of False Allegations of Child Abuse," *Penthouse*, November 1994, by permission of the author.

Before 1973, child abuse—particularly sexual abuse—was rarely reported to authorities and frequently covered up. But that year, then-Senator Walter Mondale sponsored legislation that took a new approach. Federal matching funds became available to states that set up child abuse detection, prosecution, and prevention programs. The results were startling. From 1976 to 1993, the total yearly number of child abuse reports grew from 669,000 to over 2.9 million. During the same period, the annual number of reports of sexual abuse grew from just 21,000 to over 319,000.

Undoubtedly, the increasing number of reports has saved thousands of children from harm. However, there have been some rather disturbing side-effects. In 1975, 35 percent of all child abuse reports were unsubstantiated—a percentage that, although high, was perhaps understandable given the Mondale Act's emphasis on bringing even suspicions of abuse into the open. But by 1993, the percentage of unsubstantiated reports had reached 66 percent. And in divorce cases, many experts estimate that between 75 and 80 percent of allegations of child abuse are completely false.

So what accounts for this alarming rise in false allegations? "There's a complex network of social workers, mental health professionals, and law enforcement officials that actually encourages charges of child abuse—whether they're reasonable or not," says Dr. Richard A. Gardner, a clinical professor of child psychiatry at Columbia University. In effect, the Mondale Act, despite its good intentions, created—and continues to fund—a virtual child abuse industry, populated by people whose livelihoods depend on bringing more and more allegations into the system. . . .

Whether a false allegation of abuse is made maliciously, or out of genuine concern for the welfare of a child, the result is the same for the accused. Unlike the usual "innocent until proven guilty" thing you hear about on *Perry Mason*, when it comes to child abuse, the accused is guilty until he proves himself innocent. "And that's not easy," says attorney Peter Firpo of Walnut Creek, California. "By the time a man hears he's been accused, his children have probably been seen by therapists or child protective services officers who see their role as to 'validate' the accusation." And things move pretty quickly from there: the instant the allegation is made, the father's contact with his children is cut off completely and an investigation begins.

No Pretense of Neutrality

In most states, child abuse investigations are supposed to be handled jointly by law enforcement officials and by local Child

Protective Services (CPS) workers. In general, police officers have received extensive training in investigative techniques and, at least ostensibly, are neutral. Most CPS workers, on the other hand, don't even make a pretense of neutrality. "They're advocates who seek to promote the welfare of their patients," says Dr. Lee Coleman, a child psychiatrist and frequent expert witness in child abuse cases. "They're taught to believe and support their clients—no matter what those clients say."

Dr. Gardner, who has over thirty years of experience evaluating allegations of child abuse, notes that many CPS workers refer to themselves as "validators"—a term that at best raises questions about their objectivity. "They of course hold that 'children never lie about sexual abuse,' and they accept as valid every statement a child makes that might verify sex abuse."

HOW CHILD PROTECTION TURNS ABUSIVE

With a large percentage of social workers, police officers, prosecutors, and the general public convinced that child abuse is rampant, even the remnants of due process are often swept aside. The accused is caught up in an unaccountable system. . . . Flooded with a vast number of accusations (2 million or more unsubstantiated allegations per year), the system cannot sort out the real cases from false allegations. Child protective personnel, primed to see guilt, simply grab their victims where they can.

Paul Craig Roberts, *Washington Times*, September 27, 1996.

The "believe the children" idea was popularized by Dr. Roland Summit in an influential article in the journal *Child Abuse & Neglect* in 1983. Summit wrote that "children never fabricate the kinds of explicit sexual manipulations they divulge in complaints or interrogations." Summit, who developed his theories without the benefit of any kind of scientific evidence, also claims that denial of abuse is itself frequently a sign of abuse. "If a child suspected of being abused is unable to volunteer information, it must be elicited with warm reassurance and specific, potentially leading questions."

But victims are worthless without perpetrators. So to tie the two together Summit offers this observation: "Unless there is a special support for the child and immediate intervention to force responsibility on the father, the girl will follow the 'normal' course and retract her complaint."

These approaches to child abuse allegations are based on the assumption that abuse took place—an assumption incompatible with the role of investigator, who is supposed to be neutral and determine whether a crime was committed. Despite their biased orientation, CPS's role is to determine the guilt or innocence of an accused father. This unfortunate scenario is further complicated by the fact that the police—the one potentially neutral voice in an investigation—often rely heavily on CPS's conclusions. In San Diego, for example, a Grand Jury probe found that detectives "will integrate elements of the social workers' investigation into their own reports, instead of performing an independent investigation."

The Broad Powers of CPS

In 97 percent of the cases where the police conduct an actual investigation, they are not able to substantiate the allegations, so no criminal charges are filed. But to the dismay of the thousands of men falsely accused each year, this doesn't mean that the investigation will end, or that they'll be able to see their children again anytime soon. Even after the police drop the criminal investigation, CPS can still conduct its own. And to help them do so, the courts have given them incredibly broad powers.

For example, CPS workers—armed with nothing more than an allegation, and without a court order or a hearing—can force parents and children into therapy for an unlimited amount of time, can compel an accused man to take lie detector or other "diagnostic" tests, and can deny a father access to his children—even if he has a court order allowing such access. "These are people who, at least for a limited amount of time, are given an enormous amount of power over somebody else. And they routinely abuse that power," says Dr. Melvin Guyer, a psychiatry professor at the University of Michigan and a practicing attorney.

The Role of Therapists

As part of their "investigation," CPS will frequently send a child for evaluation to an outside mental health professional selected from a court-approved list. While a skilled therapist should be able to weed out obviously false charges, by and large, the therapists to whom CPS refers children are all too willing to confirm what may actually be false reports.

In some cases, they are simply afraid to rule out abuse. To be eligible for federal funding under the Mondale Act, every state has passed laws requiring certain people (doctors, therapists, teachers, etc.) to report suspected abuse to the proper authority. To back up this requirement, these "mandated reporters" are subject to fines or imprisonment for not reporting. "As a result, everyone's on the defensive—they're afraid that if they don't make a report, they'll be deemed criminals if they inadvertently put a child back in the hands of a real abuser," says Dr. Gardner.

This fear often leads child abuse evaluators to outlandish—and tragic—conclusions. In a series of studies, Dr. Guyer and several other University of Michigan researchers presented to a panel of mental health professionals the synopsis of an actual case—one in which the researchers knew the allegation had been false. The following facts were presented: the mother had alleged abuse based on her discovery of a bruise on her two-year-old daughter's leg and of a single pubic hair (that she thought looked like the father's) in the girl's diaper. Four medical exams of the girl had shown no evidence of abuse. In addition, two lie detector tests, a police investigation, and even a CPS investigation, had cleared the father. Based on this evidence alone, 76 percent of the professionals recommended that the father's contact with the daughter be either highly supervised or terminated altogether. Several of these "child abuse experts" even managed to conclude that the girl had been sodomized as well as subjected to cunnilingus.

THERAPISTS VALIDATE FALSE REPORTS OF ABUSE

In other cases, a false report of abuse is quickly confirmed because the therapist, like the referring CPS worker, is a validator who has already made a decision before hearing what all the parties—including the father—have to say. When Dr. Gardner, who has reviewed hundreds of cases of alleged child abuse, asked various "validators" why they did not interview the father as part of their evaluation, he was frequently told, "[The father] would deny it anyway so there's no point in my seeing him," or "My job is not to do an investigation; my job is only to interview the child to find out whether the child was sexually abused."

Validators also tend to rely heavily on "behavioral and emotional indicators of abuse," which include: acting out, bed-wetting, changing attitudes about certain foods, nightmares, whining, temper tantrums, thumb-sucking, or behavior that is overly compliant or overly fearful. But these supposed "indicators" of abuse are so common, they could apply to just about anyone. "Any normal child might at some point in childhood exhibit one or more of these behaviors and thereby risk being perceived as an abuse victim," writes researcher Ross Legrand. Furthermore, many of the abuse "indicators" can also be attributed to stress and anxiety—exactly what would be experienced by a child whose parents are in a bitter divorce.

But by far the most powerful incentive to rubber-stamp an abuse charge is financial. Therapists appearing before the San Diego Grand Jury, for example, testified that they fear removal from the approved list (and, of course, a corresponding drop in income) if they "oppose the recommendations" of the CPS department. Therapists who do dare to disagree openly with the CPS worker's opinion risk "never getting to see their patient again.". . .

FRAUDULENT PHYSICAL EVIDENCE

A typical CPS investigation may also involve referring the alleged child victim for a medical exam. Some doctors, too, seem inclined to support the "findings" of the CPS workers. Like therapists, doctors may confirm abuse because they're afraid not to. And like therapists, they have financial incentives—if they don't back CPS up, they will no longer be called upon to perform evaluations.

But unlike therapists and CPS workers, who may substantiate an abuse claim based only on their opinions, doctors must generally document their reasons. However, "in medicine, statements made by patients or family are generally taken at face value," says Coleman. "So when a mother or a CPS worker sends a child to the doctor and says 'I think she's been abused by her father,' the doctor will frequently make a diagnosis of abuse based on this 'history.'"

Because sexual abuse rarely leaves any physical signs, a physical exam is not likely to give a doctor much to go on. However, a typical doctor's report will say that although no indication of abuse was found, the examination was "consistent with abuse." "Technically, there's a kernel of truth there," says Dr. Coleman. "But what gets ignored is that a normal physical exam is also consistent with no abuse. Saying 'consistent with abuse' is simply a fraud—it's language designed to help the prosecution without adding anything to the investigation."

Other times, doctors may file misleading or ambiguous reports, with disastrous results. In one disturbing case, Dr. David Gemmill, an assistant professor of pediatrics at the Medical College of Ohio, conducted an examination of a girl alleged to have been abused. In his report, Gemmill claimed to have found a "suspicious looking scar" in the little girl's anus. However, in a later review of the slides that he himself had taken during the exam, Dr. Gemmill admitted that, in fact, "there is nothing that looks suspicious." But the damage had already been done: the girl testified that the reason she believed her father had abused her was because she believed she had this scar.

Gemmill testified in court that other factors he relied on to determine that the girl had been abused—her recurring urinary tract infections and an asymmetrically shaped hymen—have been shown to be common in non-abused children.

"Nevertheless, there are doctors still basing their opinions on this type of medical misinformation," says attorney Peter Firpo. "And men are in prison because of it."

Suspicious Investigative Methods

Many CPS workers (and other child-abuse evaluators) attempt to conceal their biased methods of conducting investigations. Take, for example, their resistance to video- or audio-taping their interviews with allegedly abused children. "Just a few years ago, CPS actually advocated taping because they never even considered that what they were doing was inappropriate," says Dr. Terrence Campbell, a consulting psychologist to the Macomb County, Michigan courts. "But when other people finally got a chance to see the tapes, they saw that zealous 'professionals' were distorting the children's memories by asking leading questions. So now, there's less taping than there was even five years ago."

But even when tapes are made, they're generally inadequate. "They almost never start at the beginning of the interview, and it's usually clear that a number of interviews have already been done," says Dr. Coleman, who has reviewed over 1,100 hours of taped interviews in the cases he's worked on. "Sometimes, they interview a child until they feel they've got the child ready to say something. Only then do they turn on the tape."

One might conceivably compensate for the absence of a video- or audiotape by keeping complete, contemporaneous notes of the interview. This, however, rarely happens. Kentucky CPS worker Lisa Palmer, for example, says she makes no attempt to record her interview subjects' statements word-for-word, taking down only the "highlights." Then, after generating her final reports—in which she relies on her memory to fill in the gaps—she destroys her notes. Palmer thinks some of her coworkers do the same. . . .

Is CPS Anti-Male?

Clearly, the fear of making a mistake, combined with the financial incentives and total immunity provided by the Mondale Act, go a long way toward explaining the high number of false charges of abuse and the child abuse industry's willingness to go along with them. But some people feel that perhaps the most compelling explanation is our society's deep-rooted anti-male bias.

"There's this feeling out there that men are inherently violent and abusive, and that women and children need to be protected from them," says Dr. Guyer. "There's also an expectation that if a man hasn't already abused his children, it's only a matter of time until he does, and therefore, he shouldn't have access to them. To people who think that way, making a false allegation of abuse doesn't seem so outlandish."

Given the obvious corruption and even malicious nature of some CPS investigations, one might expect that they'd be sued quite often. But this is not the case. To be eligible for federal funding under the Mondale Act, states must pass laws protecting their mandated reporters from prosecution. "This was a pretty well-meaning provision, and it gave many people the confidence to come forward," says Dr. Gardner. "But the same immunity protects people who are making frivolous and even completely fabricated accusations.". . .

Unlike mandated reporters, ordinary people (such as vindictive ex-wives) who make false allegations can be fined or imprisoned. But as a practical matter, this rarely ever happens. "You have to prove malice, and that's almost impossible," says Kim Hart, director of the National Child Abuse Defense and Resource Center in Holland, Ohio.

THE CONSEQUENCES OF FALSE ACCUSATIONS

While anyone wrongly accused of a crime may suffer (legal fees, incarceration, etc.), those wrongly accused of abusing their children suffer far more. [One falsely accused man] has spent over $150,000 so far defending himself. Bankruptcy, unemployment, stress, health problems, alcoholism, and even suicide are not uncommon. Once accused, many men are often afraid to be alone with their—or anyone else's—children. Even men who haven't been accused, having heard about the devastation an abuse charge brings, have become afraid of being affectionate with their own children out of fear that somehow, someone will misinterpret what they're doing and they'll be dragged into the system.

Most falsely accused men find themselves in a kind of Catch-22. Despite never having been charged with any crime, they're kept away from their children because CPS continues to believe that they're guilty. The only possible way to get to see their kids would be to be exonerated in court. But because they've never been charged...

Not being able to clear one's name in court has other effects. Whenever a child abuse report is made, the alleged offender's name is entered into the Child Abuse Central Index, a national database of sex offenders. Anyone applying for a license (real-estate, child care, etc.) or undergoing a background check, will show up in the CACI as a suspected sex offender. "And when it comes to child abuse, suspected is as good as guilty. Unless a man is found not guilty in a criminal trial, or unless CPS reports that the allegation was false, the accused's name will stay on the list for life," says Hart.

Obviously, if a child has really been abused, he or she has suffered horribly. But the child put in therapy to deal with the trauma of an abuse that never happened may suffer at least as painful a fate. "Often the therapist actively fosters expressions of hostility and vengeance against the innocent parent, which may result in permanent alienation," writes Dr. Gardner. And even those rare men who are able to prevail against the false allegation may never be able to reestablish a loving relationship with their children.

Child abuse is a terrible crime, and those who abuse children should be severely punished. But in our zeal to pursue offenders, we have inadvertently created a system that itself abuses the very children we're trying so hard to protect.

"The goal of the [child protection] system is to perpetuate itself."

THE CHILD PROTECTION SYSTEM SHOULD PURSUE ALLEGATIONS OF CHILD SEXUAL ABUSE MORE AGGRESSIVELY

Leora N. Rosen and Michelle Etlin

In the following viewpoint, Leora N. Rosen and Michelle Etlin contend that social service agencies often fail to protect children from sexual abuse. Social workers, the authors claim, are given the unchallenged power to determine the validity of child abuse allegations, most of which are prematurely deemed "unfounded." Furthermore, Rosen and Etlin allege, even in the rare instance when a child abuse case is taken to court, the standards of proof make a conviction almost impossible. The authors maintain that although the child protection system deals effectively with cases of stranger molestation, it does not safeguard children from abuse occurring within the home. Rosen is a founder of Alliance for the Rights of Children and helped start Operation Z, a child advocacy organization. Etlin is the philosophical founder of Operation Z and a volunteer activist for the rights of mothers and children. They coauthored the book *The Hostage Child*, from which the following viewpoint is excerpted.

As you read, consider the following questions:

1. According to Rosen and Etlin, why may molested children recant their stories?
2. In the authors' opinion, why might a child abuse case not be prosecuted even if there is physical evidence of abuse?
3. What, in Rosen and Etlin's opinion, should be done if a child's disclosure of incest cannot be determined to be invalid?

A parent who is concerned that his or her child may have been sexually abused is likely to get the following message when calling for help:

"If you suspect sexual abuse, call this number. Someone will take your report and interview your child. If she discloses sexual abuse, they may schedule a medical evaluation to collect evidence. Then there will be an administrative finding in our agency. The case may also be referred to law enforcement for prosecution. In any case, if there has been abuse, a petition will be filed in court and you will get an order of protection or other appropriate relief to protect the child. Perhaps you should consult your lawyer."

This advice, or something similar, is offered to protective parents to show them that they will have every opportunity to obtain help for their children. Many social workers seem to believe that such a boiler-plate recitation of procedures exonerates them for the fact that the end result—protection for the child at risk—is often never reached.

The system starts with the "invitation in," which can take many forms. Children are being bombarded with public service announcements on television and programs in their schools telling them that sexual abuse is not permitted and that they should "tell" if anything suspicious is done to them. Parents are also being invited into the system by television, news reports, and announcements of a toll-free number to call if they suspect child abuse. That 800 number in turn gives out a local agency's number.

Social or "Human" Services

The first telephone call a protective adult makes on behalf of a child is to the local social service agency that is a part of county government. It may be called Welfare Department, Child Protective Services, Social Services, Family Services, Human Resources, or some similar name. (State laws require social workers, health care providers, teachers, and other professionals who work with children to report to state child protection agencies any suspicions of abuse they form from their contact with children. These are called "mandated" reports.) The telephone call is answered by an intake worker or caseworker, who has wide discretion in deciding what to do: whether to give advice, write a report and open an investigation, or unilaterally determine that there is no problem and ignore the call. If the report survives this first capricious contact, it becomes a "case" and is subjected to whatever procedures the particular agency uses to determine whether the case is valid.

Most agencies make administrative findings—within unspecified periods of time, which can drag on for months or years—and which fall into one of three categories: "founded" (meaning they believe it), "unfounded" (meaning they do not believe it), or the very dangerous "undetermined" (meaning they do not know and seemingly do not care). Social service agencies intervene only in cases labeled "founded"; and intervention means that the agency takes the case to court. There, a single judge can decide whether or not to believe the administrative finding. A judge who disbelieves the finding can rule that there is "no credible evidence," and that case is as good as "unfounded."

What steps lead to the agency finding? There is no standard answer to this question. Usually, the child is interviewed by agency personnel. The child's own therapist, mother, doctor, and other trusted significant adults may be completely ignored; the child is usually expected to repeat her disclosures to a stranger interviewing her on behalf of the agency. The interviewer does not need to follow any particular procedure. Social workers are subjected to rigorous cross-examination about their conclusions only if they do in fact believe a child and go to court to support the allegations. If, however, they disbelieve the allegations—regardless of the reason—their conclusion is automatically accepted as the basis for an unfounded case and their rationale is not challenged. If one worker believes an allegation, the child is sometimes interviewed by other workers. Some children have been subjected to as many as fourteen interviews. As long as they continue to disclose, they stay on the treadmill; but the first time they fail to disclose, the case is marked as a "recant" and considered unfounded. If, after a recant, a child returns to the original story, the disclosure is considered "inconsistent" and thus unfounded. In the face of multiple interviews, most molested children will recant at some point because the sheer volume of interrogation leads them to feel that their disclosures are not being believed. Molested children, who are especially insecure, are very vulnerable to such tactics and may recant at some point because they feel threatened in general.

THE ROLE OF PHYSICAL EVIDENCE IN PROSECUTING CASES

If an interviewer believes the child's disclosure, there will generally be a search for physical evidence. In 80 percent of all real cases of sexual abuse, however, there is no physical evidence of the act. Only the presence of semen in a child's body, or unhealed evidence of forcible penetration of the genitals of a girl whose hymen was previously proven to be intact, can rise to the level of "solid evidence," and there are very few such cases. Research shows that the sexual abuse of young children usually consists of acts that do not leave clear physical signs: oral sex, "fondling," partial penetration, sodomy, forced fellatio, digital penetration. A multitude of such acts can be perpetrated upon a child many times and leave nothing for physicians to identify. Even if a child is afflicted with a sexually transmitted disease, it is rarely possible to identify its origin because the perpetrator may have sought treatment before the child's symptoms are identified. More often than not, then, the results of the search for forensic evidence results in a lack of findings or, at most, a finding that is called "consistent with but not conclusive of" sexual abuse. Unfortunately, the translation from medical to legal terms subtly changes the semantics of this kind of finding. What a doctor calls "consistent" but "not conclusive" is often described by the lawyers as "inconclusive" and leads judges to conclude illogically that the finding really means "no abuse."

RISE IN CHILD ABUSE IN THE U.S.

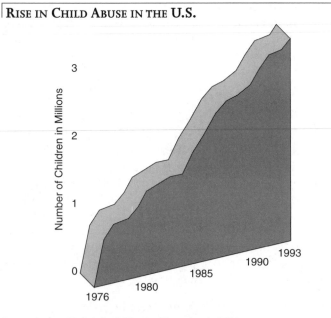

Source: Andrew Vachss, *Parade Magazine*, November 3, 1996.

If medical findings firmly support the conclusion that the child has been molested, the agency generally involves the police and/or prosecutor. Unfortunately, that can create more problems than it solves. Police do not look at a case in terms of child protection; that is someone else's job. They are interested in whether their prosecutor will take the case to court, and so they look at the potential weaknesses of a case, not at the evidence. They may ask, for instance, whether the child has ever masturbated, in case the defense lawyer tries to explain away physical evidence by suggesting that she penetrated herself. Such questions frighten many children and cause them to become "not a good witness," which would be fatal to a prosecution. Prosecutors determine whether to press charges by measuring their chances of winning, not on whether they believe the crime has been committed. Since criminal proceedings require "proof beyond a reasonable doubt," and since most prosecutors are not eager to add losing cases to their balance sheets, they refuse to prosecute incest cases if they have any of the following weaknesses: victim under ten years old; "conflicting information" developed in the multiple interviews; a perpetrator who is already accusing the protective parent of "false allegations in a custody dispute." Prosecutors can refuse to take a case for any reason or for no reason at all and are under no obligation to prosecute.

Most prosecutors prefer cases against stepfathers or mothers' boyfriends to those against biological fathers. The odds against a successful prosecution of a biological father for incest are almost unsurmountable unless he admits guilt.

The fact that a prosecutor decides not to prosecute is often flaunted as evidence that the allegations were "false." Time after time, social workers who have supported children's disclosures have been pressured to change their positions after prosecutions have been dropped because of "insufficient evidence." Of course, this confuses law enforcement purposes (convictions) with social service purposes (child protection), but the reality is that a failed or abandoned prosecution usually results in a rebound that drives the social services agency off the case forever.

STANDARD OF PROOF IN COURT

Lay persons often assume that a judicial decision to protect a child from the risk of sexual abuse is equivalent to finding a defendant guilty as charged, while a decision against protecting a child is the same as finding a defendant innocent. A few years ago, a man at a Free Elizabeth Morgan rally loudly insisted that the judge had "found the father innocent." That was not true. Eric Foretich was never tried for sexual abuse of his daughter in either a criminal court or a child-abuse proceeding; the District of Columbia court ruled only on the custody issue. The judge had not found Foretich "innocent"; he had simply granted the father's request for visitation. [During a custody battle, Elizabeth Morgan had accused former husband Eric Foretich of abusing their daughter. She refused to follow the judge's order that Foretich be allowed unsupervised visits with his daughter and was consequently sent to jail.] People frequently misunderstand the differences between criminal and civil proceedings as well as whose rights and which rights are at stake if the wrong decision is made. Advocates for alleged molesters mention with horror the idea that lengthy prison sentences can be imposed on the basis of flimsy evidence or children's lies. But seldom do we hear about the standards of evidence required to ensure a child's right to protection from possible rape, even when the alleged molester is not being criminally charged. A certain circular reasoning is involved: if the alleged molester is not charged with or not found guilty of a crime, he is innocent; and if he is innocent, the child needs no protection. That analysis fails to take into account the possibility that a child needs protection even when there is not enough evidence to put an alleged molester in jail—which is most often the case. The confusion is compounded by the fact that in the three different kinds of possible proceedings (criminal, child abuse, and custody), there are three different standards of proof.

Criminal Proceedings. Child sexual abuse is a crime. Cases involving incest by a biological father are rarely prosecuted. The social service agency may decide that it would be harmful for the child to testify or that a trial would not help the family. If there is prosecution, the standard of evidence is proof beyond a reasonable doubt—a very heavy evidentiary standard.

Civil Proceedings: Child Abuse. The county attorney, not the prosecutor, usually decides whether an alleged molester will be charged with child abuse, child neglect, or something called "endangerment" in a civil proceeding. The county attorney also represents another powerful client, the social service agency. In an abuse hearing, the standard before a family court judge—not a jury—is "clear and convincing evidence" that abuse did occur, at a particular time, in a particular way. A judge may call the evidence "not convincing" merely because he is not convinced. Judge Gordon Mitchell of Dade County, Florida stated on TV that he was upset by being asked to rule against a father who was a professor of political science at Miami University. He characterized his problem as being asked to "say that somebody put his penis . . . in somebody else's tush!" For that, he said, "the evidence has to be conclusive, and I looked at it, and it was not conclusive." The evidence that he "looked at" included a boy's disclosure that his father had molested him; statements from two psychologists that they believed he had been molested; a police officer who believed the boy had been sexually assaulted; the Children's Services Division, which believed the boy had been sexually assaulted; and the opinion of the medical director of the Miami rape treatment center, who had examined a tear to the child's anus and concluded that the boy had been sodomized. But Judge Mitchell was not convinced. Obviously, there is no definition of what constitutes "clear and convincing" evidence.

Civil Proceedings: Custody. In a custody case, the standard is not "clear and convincing" evidence but a "preponderance of the evidence," meaning 51 percent. In the Morgan-Foretich case, Judge Herbert Dixon ordered Morgan to send her daughter on a six-week unsupervised visit with her father while the evidence that the child had been raped by her father was "in equipoise." Equipoise is 50/50—one percentage point short of tipping the scale for a preponderance. In other words, Judge Dixon, believing there was a 50 percent chance that the child Hilary had been raped on a previous visit, ordered that the 50 percent risk of rape be repeated for six weeks. If she and her mother had not left the country, the judge could have decided custody on the 50/50 line he had mentally drawn between protection of the child and the right of the father to have unsupervised access to her.

Who Is the Defendant? When William Kennedy Smith was acquitted of charges of rape, constitutional law expert Alan Dershowitz said on television that the complaining witness should be charged with perjury for making false allegations against the accused rapist. If "reasonable doubt" can be expressed as 10 percent doubt, Smith might have been acquitted because a jury could not conclude, with 90 percent certainty, that he had raped the witness. It does not mean that the alleged victim was 90 percent wrong about being raped. And if there was a 10 percent chance that she had perjured herself, that would not even rise to what is called a *prima facie* case (enough evidence for a prosecution to go forward). Yet one of the nation's most highly respected criminal lawyers made the illogical suggestion, which was accepted by many Americans as a reasonable and rational idea, that something had been proven false by failing to have been proven true.

With regard to incest allegations, the system sets up an unreasonable standard of proof. When it is not met, the same system maintains no standard to presume wrong-doing on the part of the protective parent or complaining child witness and creates confusion as to who is the actual defendant in a child sexual abuse case. The confusion is not merely the result of a leap of logic; it is also the result of failure to realize who should have the lion's share of constitutional protection. Although the child is not a defendant in the traditional legal sense, the position of any child at risk of incest is equivalent to that of a defendant in terms of loss of liberty if the judge errs on the side of the alleged molester. If one is not sure, beyond a reasonable doubt, that a child's disclosure of incest is invalid, it should be presumed valid, the child should be presumed innocent of making a false allegation, and the child should be protected.

The Criminal/Civil Abuse/Custody Court Shuffle. With or without prosecution, a social services agency will go to court for a protective parent and child only if it has firmly made, and continues to support, a founded case of sexual abuse against the named perpetrator. If it has chosen to call the case "undetermined" or "unfounded," it is just as likely to go to court against the protective parent, either in a "disposition" hearing in the abuse case or in a custody case, and testify that the parent tried to get them to substantiate sexual abuse—as if that were a crime or evidence of parental unfitness.

This point in the process is the most dangerous to the protective parent, even if travel through the social service maze has been successful so far. If one court is empowered to hear abuse and another is empowered to hear custody, the case may be transferred; then evidence of abuse may not be admissible because the case is not in the right court to hear about it. As though abuse were not relevant to custody determinations, judges often rule that if a prior court proceeding hearing abuse was transferred or consolidated into the custody forum, the transfer effectively prevents the "contestants for custody" from using evidence of abuse developed in the other court. Therefore, by the simple expedient of suing for custody in the midst of a child-abuse trial, an alleged molester can whisk the evidence into no-man's-land, as the custody judge will not hear it and the abuse judge has given up jurisdiction to hear it. Without cooperation from the social service agency or the county attorney (who represents the social service agency), the protective parent cannot prevent this kind of legalistic sleight of hand from destroying a perfectly valid child-protection proceeding.

Worse yet, the fact that the protective parent believed that there was sexual abuse can now be used against her in a custody proceeding (called "interference with visitation" or "antispousal behavior"), whereas the valid reasons for her belief are excluded from the proceedings. Since she cannot adduce the evidence that would show she had a sound reason to believe her child was molested, she is left without a defense against the charge that she deliberately tried to alienate the child from the father, against whom, by now—at least in this court—there is "no evidence."

A FAILED SYSTEM

After a case has been examined by social services, bounced around through county government, examined by professionals, subjected to the vagaries of prosecutors and courts, and handled and mishandled by lawyers, it is almost impossible to pinpoint where in the system things went wrong. Even narrating and documenting such a case becomes nearly insurmountable because at any juncture there can be half a dozen twists. It would take a person of enormous strength to get through this maze and still remain calm and in control at all times, especially if her child is at risk or, worse yet, still being abused. As a result, "mistakes" pile up that are later charged against the protective parent: she should not have said this, she should not have done that, she should have gone to a different doctor, hired a different lawyer, made sure a certain subpoena was issued, made a particular call, not made that call, etc., etc., *ad nauseam*.

At the end of this travail, most victimized mothers and their advocates mistakenly identify one piece of the puzzle as "the problem," often picking the moment when they were the most shocked or astounded. One mother insists that interviews should be videotaped because children are often intimidated; another thinks that medical examinations should always be done with colposcopes so photographs can record the results; another wants judges hearing custody cases to be required to consider certain kinds of evidence; another believes that prosecutors should be legally required to issue whatever subpoenas the complaining witnesses demand. Although all these arguments can lead to attempts to change the law or pass new ones designed to make the system work, the impassioned and fragmented responses of victims and their bedraggled advocates have never changed the big picture.

We argue that the system is in fact working—in the way it has chosen to work. No matter which adjustment we support, it will continue to do what it chooses in response. The political and practical reality is that the goal of the system is to perpetuate itself and the policies, written and unwritten, by which it has already chosen to operate.

The system as we have outlined it appears capricious at best and unreliable at worst. This does not mean, however, that children are never protected from sexual abuse. It is important to remember that our overview is applicable primarily to incest cases, or cases of intra-familial sexual abuse. A somewhat different set of principles applies in cases involving stranger molesters. Some steps in the system are the same for both kinds of cases, but others differ, depending on the identity and legal rights of the named perpetrators. Strangers do not have inalienable rights over a child and cannot sue for custody. Even in criminal court, different procedures are used, and these, in turn, affect civil proceedings. For example, a biological father accused of molesting his own child is usually given an exculpatory polygraph by the prosecutor's office. If he doesn't want to submit to the test, or if he takes it and fails, that is not used against him, since the test is not admissible as evidence. However, if he passes the test the charges against him are usually dismissed immediately. Strangers accused of molesting children are not given the same courtesy.

The bottom line is that a child is more likely to be protected by the system from a stranger molester (from whom his own parents can protect him) than from an incest perpetrator.

> "Children involved in parental abuse cases often [take] advantage of their power in court proceedings to fabricate sexual abuse."

CHILDREN LIE ABOUT CHILD SEXUAL ABUSE

Hans Sebald

In the following viewpoint, Hans Sebald maintains that the modern-day fervor to uncover child abusers is similar to the panic about witches during the sixteenth and seventeenth centuries; both scares, he claims, were initiated by children's ludicrous accusations and perpetuated by the belief that "children don't lie." According to Sebald, some children are extremely prone to lying and inventing fantastical stories of abuse, especially when prodded by the leading questions of interviewers. Sebald is professor emeritus of sociology at Arizona State University.

As you read, consider the following questions:

1. In Sebald's opinion, why do children engage in mythomania?
2. According to the author, how might concerned adults unknowingly encourage children to lie about abuse?
3. How have the mass media encouraged false child abuse allegations, according to Sebald?

Reprinted from Hans Sebald, "Witch-Children: The Myth of the Innocent Child," *Issues in Child Abuse Accusations*, vol. 9, no. 3/4, pp. 179–86, by permission of the Institute for Psychological Therapies.

"The innocence of the little ones" is a phrase of dubious veracity, since historical events suggest otherwise. Nowhere has this optimism stumbled over more obstinate obstacles than during the witch-hunts of the sixteenth and seventeenth centuries. During those not-so-distant years vast numbers of children gave free rein to imagination and played back the image of the witch with such zeal that they substantially contributed to the persecution. Without any compunction did they denounce and bring to the stake uncounted thousands of innocent persons. Their victims were old and young, men and women, playmates, and even members of their immediate families. . . .

Researchers have just recently become more fully aware that in the majority of witch panics children were responsible for starting the hysteria, fueling it with the wildest of allegations, and completing it with lethal accusations. Children played a pivotal role, linking the power of the inquisitor or the judge to the fates of a variety of people. It is this nexus that is overdue for scientific examination. The question arises whether this type of child behavior was merely an expression of an aberrant Zeitgeist, of an era of theological fanaticism, or whether it was an expression of a timeless condition found in the child's psyche.

THE NEW WITCH-HUNT

Evidently the children's destructive behavior cannot be put aside as a neatly encapsulated phenomenon of an erring era, because the classical Salem syndrome is anything but past history: It is an ongoing process. Children again are the masters of the nexus between prosecutor and defendant. This time the accused are not called witches but molesters or abusers, and a new panic of epidemic proportion is underway.

There are, of course, significant differences between the two maniacal hunts. Most importantly, child molestation is an unfortunate fact of life. It's not fictional, it happens. On the other hand, witchcraft—certainly in form of its assumed effectuality—was a figment of the theological imagination. Extremely few of the accused had ever tried their wits in the black arts, and yet the persecutions proceeded with the utmost certainty that they had—a prejudged certainty as we see it again emerge in the persecution of presumed child molesters today. Persons eager to persecute frequently seem to forget that such claims can be true or false. Hence the great art today is to learn to distinguish between false and true accusations. Perhaps a better understanding of child psychology can help in this matter.

Modern situations in which children can wreak tragedy include court proceedings where children are stimulated to tune into a theme and harmonize with it. They often pick up cues how to harmonize with leading questions—questions that are not meant to be leading but cannot withstand the intuitive exploitation by perceptive children. Fertile ground for abusing the abuse-accusation are court situations dealing with divorce and the custody of minor children, and the molestation-accusation of teachers, especially of preschool teachers. Children are well endowed with intuitive acuity to figure out what is to their advantage and how to cater to suggestive questions. And some children are veritable virtuosi in doing so.

Mythomania and Child Testimony

This is where the concept of "mythomania" comes into play. This mania to make up myths is also known by the technical term "pseudologia phantastica" and refers to a person's compulsive lying and making up fantastic stories. This phrase originated with experts in forensic medicine who had opportunity to observe children giving false testimony. Psychiatrists discovered that a mythomane may initially lie deliberately and consciously, but gradually come to believe in what he or she is saying. The vast majority of persons engaging in such confabulation were children or the mentally retarded.

Interestingly, experts have found that lying by children does not necessarily indicate a chronic pathology and is not classified as mental illness, whereas it is if it persists in adults. Children have an incomplete grasp of the contours of the real world and often resort to making up stories if they are under pressure or if they sense that such stories are expected. When they do make up stories they can be motivated by a variety of reasons. Many engage in mythomania to gain attention and praise, some use it to satisfy precocious sexual appetites, some revel in the power it affords them, and some use it as a vehicle of pure malice. In situations where mythomanes are motivated by attention-seeking, they are particularly susceptible to suggestion. With a flair for figuring out what is expected, they set out on their mythomaniacal journey, during which compelling autosuggestion evolves, with the storytellers programming their brains to confer reality status to the stories. Ultimately it is no longer a question of the child lying; the child starts to believe in the reality of the story.

The material children use to build imaginative structures frequently consists of what they glean from adult conversations. Mythomaniacal children seek suggestions; their radar, as it were, is constantly scanning the social horizon for cues to spin stories rewarding them recognition. Theirs is the skill to quickly evaluate what they overhear and use it to advantage—and sometimes to the detriment of others, innocent or guilty.

This skill, in addition to verbal expressivity, enables mythomanes to tune into a theme with persuasive loquacity. Through confabulation and strategic gossiping they can humor people's biases and expectations with such effectiveness that their utterances are accepted as true revelations. . . .

THE SUGGESTIBILITY OF CHILDREN

The key element in mythomania . . . is *suggestibility*. Observers on the modern scene have witnessed the creation of mythomaniacal profusion during numerous court hearings dealing with claims of child molestation. They noticed how a biased and one-sided climate was created through the unconscious collaboration of the questioner and the child, whereby the child emerged as if a proven victim of perverse crime.

In the majority of cases, concerned adults, particularly parents, showed anxiousness to know all about the assault—its nature, time, place, motive, and so on. The child may initially have been bewildered and embarrassed by all the questions—a reaction interpreted by the questioner, or the court, as a sign of shame. Right away the child would be inundated by encouraging words and leading questions. The child would follow the lead and answer in a way to meet the more or less obvious expectations of the questioners. The hearing would turn into a rehearsal of a story that the child now learned by heart. In future rehearsals, the child stuck to the version now imprinted in his or her mind. The only changes the child might make consisted of adding new material conforming to this version.

The majority of the cases included claims of sexual abuse. Research by psychologists David Raskin and Phillip Esplin found that children involved in parental abuse cases often took advantage of their power in court proceedings to fabricate sexual abuse in order to punish one parent or side with the other. The researchers noted that such distortion was a strong tendency when divorce, custody, or visitation disputes were involved. . . .

REASONS FOR CHILD SUGGESTIBILITY

While research into the actual forensic problems proved to be extremely difficult, a number of psychologists have chosen laboratory situations in an attempt to identify the principles underlying children's vulnerability to influence and manipulation. While the findings are far from complete, several insights have been gained.

Suggestibility varies with age. Psychologist Maria Zaragosa found that young children (under eight) have greater difficulty than older children and adults in distinguishing between imagined events and those they actually experienced. "Given the greater tendency to confuse imagination with perception, young children might also be more likely to confuse items that were merely suggested to them with those they had actually perceived."

If, however, intrusion of extraneous information and the posing of leading questions are avoided—thus creating a sort of cognitively sterile environment for the child—children's recall of factual material has been found to be amazingly accurate, approaching in quality that of adults. Research data show that, according to H.R. Dent, "children are capable of being good eyewitnesses, but that their recall appears to be more vulnerable to various distorting influences in the interview situation than does adult recall."

Once a child begins a course of confabulation, a process of self-brainwashing snaps into action. Self-brainwashing differs from brainwashing, as the former starts with voluntary confabulation and gradually assumes truth value in the mind of the narrator. The latter starts with external pressure to persuade a person to change his or her mind and ends with a new orientation.

DO CHILDREN LIE?

Studies on the truth value of children's verbalizations have been conducted at the Institute for the Study of Child Development at the University of Medicine of New Jersey. It was discovered that already at age three a majority of children will lie in certain situations. When the liars were challenged, only 38% of them admitted to having lied, with boys more likely than girls admitting their dishonesty. Another study found that deception can often be detected by unconscious body movements that differ from the person's normal movements. However, according to R.L. Jahn, such differentiating body language was missing in "pathological liars or those who simply feel no remorse about lying." Findings of this nature bear on the credibility of children's testimony and accusations in more than one way. First, they remind us that children may lie; second, they proffer the disturbing fact that liars and truth-tellers cannot easily be told apart.

A revealing study identified some of the dangers that may arise from children's reports. Psychologists Karen Saywitz and Gail Goodman interviewed 72 girls, ages five and seven, about routine medical procedures they had received. Half were given full examination, including vaginal and anal checks; the rest were given just general physicals. When the first group was asked broad and nonspecific questions about the procedure, only eight mentioned the vaginal checks, and when the children were shown anatomically correct dolls, six pointed to the vaginal area. But of the girls who had undergone a merely general checkup, three claimed they also had had vaginal or anal examinations; one child even said that "a doctor did it with a stick."

HOW INTERVIEWERS PRODUCE FALSE TESTIMONY

• Interviewers often ask leading questions, questions that suggest a particular answer, such as "Did he touch your privates?" Such questions are more likely to elicit an incriminating response than nonsuggestive questions, such as "What did he do next?"

• When children deny having been molested, interviewers often repeat the question. When this happens, children are likely to conclude that their original denial was the "wrong answer" and switch to an affirmative response.

• Interviewers sometimes negatively stereotype the suspect by referring to the suspect as a bad person or someone who does bad things. This increases the likelihood that the child will make an accusation.

• When interviewers selectively reinforce accusations of abuse with attention and praise while ignoring denials, the child will repeat and expand upon those accusations.

• When children are told that their peers have already reported incidents of abuse by the suspect, they are more likely to accuse the suspect as well.

Lloyd K. Stires, *Gauntlet*, Vol. II, 1996.

Most of the claims of abuse and the resulting trials involve day care centers, preschools, and divorce/custody disputes. The most frequent charges of sexual abuse occur as a part of custody quarrels. According to estimates, the charge is raised in about 5% of child-custody cases. A 1988 study by the Association of Family and Conciliation Courts concluded the charges probably are false 30–40% of the time. Hollida Wakefield and Ralph Underwager researched the psychological profile of the accusers (mostly parents using their children's testimony) and discovered that 74% of the falsely accusing parents were afflicted with personality disorders. Regardless of their problems, they usually are successful in using sex-molestation charges as a strategy to obtain custody and to achieve revenge against former spouses. The children become pawns in the process, and the opponents vie for their cooperation. The party winning is usually the one that is more successful in manipulating the children.

MODERN DAY WITCH-HUNTS

This brings to mind a disturbing parallelism between patterns of the past witch-hunt and patterns of the present court proceedings. In both scenarios children were often asked to report on their family life, especially whether it incorporated elements deviating from acceptable standards. And in both situations children catered to the inquisitiveness of the authority figures in order to be appreciated and made to feel important.

Increasing numbers of preschools have become the target of child molestation charges. One dealt with a San Diego Sunday school teacher, Dale Akiki, whom nine children accused of rape, sodomy, and torture. The drawn-out court hearings heard the children's claims that the teacher had killed a baby, sacrificed rabbits, and slaughtered an elephant and a giraffe. The jury in the Superior Court concluded that the children weren't credible and acquitted Akiki—after he had spent two and a half years behind bars. . . .

A most destructive version of the genre took its fateful course in 1983 at a preschool in Manhattan Beach, California. Two teachers at the McMartin preschool, Peggy Buckey, 63, and her son Raymond, 31, were accused by Judy Johnson, the mother of a two-and-one-half-year-old boy, of having molested her son. Thereupon a public hysteria spread, resembling old Salem, and soon 41 children were involved and 208 counts filed against seven individuals.

Johnson's complaints against the teachers grew bizarre. Later, as the investigation was still underway, Johnson was diagnosed an acute paranoid schizophrenic and died of alcohol-related liver disease. But by then the prosecution had stirred up enough other witnesses and felt no need to revise the initial witness's testimony. The police had written to 200 parents announcing their investigation of sexual abuse at the preschool, thereby fanning the hysteria and encouraging more children to come forth with lurid tales of abuse.

SUGGESTIVE INTERVIEWING TECHNIQUES

An administrator-turned-therapist soon established that 369 of the 400 children she interviewed had been abused. Her technique was blatantly suggestive—she gave emotional rewards to the children who accused the teachers, and rebuffs to those who did not. "What good are you? You must be dumb," she said to one child who knew nothing about the game Naked Movie Star. The collection of stories she presented to the authorities as being credible included children digging up dead bodies at cemeteries; being taken for rides in airplanes; killing animals (including a horse) with bats; observing devil worship; being buried alive; seeing naked priests cavorting in a secret cellar below the school; seeing a teacher fly; having been given red or pink liquids to make them sleepy. Reminiscent of the denunciations made by children at witch trials during past centuries, the preschool children identified a number of members of the community as they were driven around town and asked to point out molesters. The children pointed out community leaders, store clerks, gas-station attendants; one child picked out photos of actor Chuck Norris and Los Angeles City Attorney James Hahn. . . .

Peggy Buckey and her son Raymond . . . suffered the longest criminal trial in American history. It was not until 1990 that they were acquitted—after they had spent two years and five years, respectively, in jail.

There is a frightening story to be told about the power of the mass media. The California episode was exploited by the media and produced a tremendous repercussion across the nation—not one of caution, as one might have expected, but one of ever larger numbers of children imitating similar claims. As M. Carlson states, "Nationally, the attention generated by the case set off an explosion of reports claiming sexual abuse of children, increasing such reports from 6,000 in 1976 to an estimated 350,000 in 1988." The main responsibility for the explosion must be placed on the mass media which wallowed in lurid detail. The perils created by the media's suggestive force include increasing numbers of parents and authorities using the malleable power of children to bring about testimonies serving biases and schemes of partisan adults. As someone warned: "Some parents, determined to damage each other in a divorce, are throwing abuse charges around. Those bent on destroying a reputation have a surefire weapon." This modern "surefire weapon" is the equivalent of the witch accusation of past times; again it is based on the testimony of children, a testimony whose truth value is hard to prove or disprove, but still a testimony too often credulously accepted.

"Rarely . . . would a preschooler be motivated to lie about something as traumatic as sexual abuse."

CHILDREN DO NOT LIE ABOUT CHILD SEXUAL ABUSE

Sylvia Lynn Gillotte

Sylvia Lynn Gillotte alleges in the following viewpoint that children have the capacity to testify honestly and accurately about incidents of child abuse. She claims that current research shows that children are not as suggestible as is commonly believed; furthermore, she contends, even very young children have demonstrated the ability to differentiate between fact and fantasy. Gillotte is an attorney for the South Carolina Office of the Governor. She is also chairman of the South Carolina Bar Resource Manual Project on representing children in family court.

As you read, consider the following questions:

1. According to Gillotte, why might young children need memory cues when testifying?
2. What, in the author's opinion, is the relationship between age and suggestibility?
3. What is the most common lie that occurs in sexual abuse cases, according to Gillotte?

Reprinted, by permission, from Sylvia Lynn Gillotte, "The Child Witness," in *Representing Children in Family Court: A Resource Manual for Attorneys and Guardians ad Litem*, published by the South Carolina Bar at http://childlaw.law.sc.edu/resourcemanual (cited May 29, 1998).

Historically, legal rules concerning the competency of witnesses have always been a reflection of social assumptions and values. Thus, for many years, slaves, women and children were not allowed to testify in court. Under common law, it was generally believed that children under the age of fourteen were incompetent to testify as witnesses in court. This rule was based upon the rebuttable presumption that a child did not have the capacity and intelligence to relate information accurately and was not capable of understanding the difference between the truth under sworn testimony and a lie.

Consequently, any child which an attorney wished to present as a witness had to first pass a competency examination prior to testifying. In 1895, the Supreme Court set down the guidelines for modern competency examinations in its decision in *Wheeler v. United States* [159 U.S. 523 (1895)]. The Court established a three-pronged test which is still used by jurisdictions requiring competency examinations:

1) *Capacity and intelligence.* At the time the testimony is offered, the child must have the capacity to receive accurate impressions of the facts to which the testimony relates; sufficient memory to retain an independent recollection of the impression; and the ability to accurately communicate the impressions, including understanding the questions posed and framing intelligent answers.

2) *Distinguishing between the truth and a lie.* The child must be able to distinguish between the truth and a lie, fact and fantasy.

3) *Appreciating the duty to tell the truth.* In addition to understanding the difference between the truth and a lie, the child must be able to demonstrate that he or she understands the nature of the oath to tell the truth and the consequences should he or she fail to do so.

Once a child was determined to meet the above requisites, he or she could testify, regardless of his or her particular age.

UNFAIR COMPETENCY LAWS

Following the *Wheeler* decision, many states passed laws which only presumed competency in children over the age of fourteen. Unfortunately, so many courts began excluding the testimony of children under the age of fourteen that it became the number one barrier to successful prosecution of child sexual molestation cases.

In recognition of the unfairness and impracticality of competency rules, the 1974 revision of the Federal Rules of Evidence abolished these rules in favor of allowing the testimony of virtually every witness in Federal Court. Many states have modified their own rules accordingly, and others have passed laws that require courts to presume the competency of child witnesses. . . .

MEMORY AND RECALL

Historically, children have been perceived as unreliable, unbelievable, and unable to distinguish between fact and fiction. This was particularly true of children under the age of five or six. Throughout the last two decades, however, numerous clinical studies have been done which have modified our understanding of children's memory and recall as well as their ability to testify accurately in court.

Studies conducted by various researchers indicate that when certain guidelines are followed which correspond to the child's level of development, even very young children have the capacity to testify quite accurately regarding their experiences. In general, they are able to relate both familiar and novel events, as well as stressful and non-stressful events. Understandably, children are most accurate concerning events they have participated in or personally experienced, rather than observed.

Young children do apparently differ in their ability to respond to questions involving "free recall." Free recall involves remembering an event without the assistance of memory cues and is considered a complex cognitive process and form of memory retrieval. Consequently, although their memory of an event may be accurate, young children might require a memory cue in order to retrieve the memory when questioned or testifying. They might also have more difficulty responding to open-ended questions.

IMPROVING CHILD TESTIMONY

It is critical to remember that children are most able to testify accurately in an atmosphere which is relaxed and non-threatening, something not often evident in a courtroom setting. Therefore, consideration should be given to providing an alternative setting for the child, or minimizing any perceived threats. With young children, this might be accomplished by requesting that the child be permitted to testify in the lap of a supportive adult or holding a favorite toy. In some cases, it necessitates that the court take all necessary steps to ensure that the child is not forced to face his or her perpetrator while testifying.

As with adults, the passage of time takes its toll on memory. However, because children are more likely to focus on the core event of an experience and are less likely to remember and relate specific details, delay in the taking of testimony can be detrimental when dealing with a child witness. Therefore, in most cases, it is appropriate to request that a child's testimony be taken and preserved early if the adjudication hearing is not likely to be held within a reasonable time.

Another final point to remember is that certain interviewing techniques can improve children's ability to recall the details of events. Assisting the child through mental reconstruction can be very helpful.

SUGGESTIBILITY

Though many adults believe that children are highly suggestible, current research is eroding this premise. Recent psychological studies which focus on realistic and personally meaningful events, and which thereby have more forensic significance, reveal that children are much more resistant to suggestibility than previously thought.

There appears to be no clear relationship between age and suggestibility, which depends more upon the cognitive, emotional, social and situational factors involving the subject. Therefore, children are not always more suggestible than adults. And while extremely young children may be slightly more suggestible than older children, the fact remains that the area most subject to suggestibility deals with peripheral details in memory retrieval.

As memory and recall of peripheral details fails, then suggestibility increases. This can be said about adults as well as children. However, a child being asked to interpret an ambiguous event, or who is questioned about an event that was merely observed rather than experienced, is more suggestible than a child being questioned about the "facts" of an event which was personally experienced.

On the other hand, studies have also shown that there is a risk in not asking suggestive questions when the situation in question relates to an experience which is embarrassing and sensitive. For example, occasional use of mildly suggestive questions might be necessary to elicit truthful and accurate testimony regarding sexual abuse. The shame, fear and threats that a child might be experiencing hinder the child's ability to be open and feel safe. Therefore, some flexibility in the examination process is called for, especially in the area of sexual abuse or molestation.

DIFFERENTIATING FACT FROM FANTASY

Studies have shown us that children understand the difference between truth and falsehood, even when they don't understand the word "difference," which is often the case in children under five. There is absolutely no evidence that children lie more than adults; however, when they do lie, they are not as proficient as adults in doing so. In fact, the older the child, the more proficient he or she becomes at relating falsehoods. Young children, in particular, have difficulty maintaining conscious fabrication over a period of time.

CHILDREN CAN PROVIDE RELIABLE TESTIMONY

Children are often portrayed as unreliable witnesses, susceptible to suggestive or misleading questions and incapable of accurately or completely recalling details. A growing body of research shows that even two- and three-year-olds can remember and report personally experienced events as accurately as adults. If investigators ask the right questions to stimulate and guide efforts to retrieve memories, children can provide complete, reliable information.

National Center for Prosecution of Child Abuse, July/August 1995.

In assessing either a child's or an adult's veracity, it is important to ask what factors might motivate that particular individual to lie. Preschoolers, for example, have very simple and limited motivations for lying which can usually be readily discerned. A preschooler might lie to express an intense desire or wish, to avoid punishment, or perhaps to please a parent. Rarely, however, would a preschooler be motivated to lie about something as traumatic as sexual abuse. Furthermore, any untruth about such an experience would be offset by his or her inability to sustain the falsehood under questioning.

Both children and adults fantasize and daydream, and while imagination and fantasy are an important part of children's lives, studies have shown that children can separate what they experience from what they imagine. It would be highly unlikely for a young child to fantasize that he or she had been physically or sexually abused, especially with limited experience and knowledge of sexuality. Certainly, if reasonable doubt is in the mind of the interviewer, then careful and considered questioning which is unfettered by a bias will usually reveal the truth.

Our society has long held misconceptions about children and their credibility and competency to testify in judicial proceedings. This is particularly true in the area of sexual abuse, where denial of the problem is rampant, even among jurists. In his book *On Trial: America's Courts and Their Treatment of Sexually Abused Chil-*

dren, Judge Charles B. Schudson writes:

> Children do not commonly make false claims of being sexually abused. Under-reporting and denial are far more common. . . . The veracity of sexually abused children has been analyzed by researchers, all of whom report that false accusations are extremely rare... The adult notion that children lie is illogical to those who have studied them closely. [Charles B. Schudson & Billie Wright Dziech, *On Trial: America's Courts and Their Treatment of Sexually Abused Children*, 2d ed. (Beacon Press 1991), at 57.]

THE LIE OF RETRACTION

In reality, the most common lie which occurs in sexual abuse cases is that of retraction. Retraction, or subsequent denial of a previously disclosed allegation, is one of the elements discussed in "The Child Sexual Abuse Accommodation Syndrome," by Dr. Roland Summitt [in *Child Abuse & Neglect* 177 (1983)]. Retraction is common and predictable in cases involving sexual abuse; and when it occurs, it may be advisable to bring in an expert witness who can discuss the Child Sexual Abuse Accommodation Syndrome to rehabilitate the child's initial disclosure(s). While testimony concerning retraction and other elements of the CSAAS cannot be offered to prove sexual abuse, it can be introduced to explain inconsistencies, retractions, and delayed disclosures.

Retraction is just one of the reactive behaviors frequently seen in victims of sexual abuse. Because children are either fearful of their abusers, or fearful of the consequences to both themselves and their abusers following disclosure, they usually keep the secret of their sexual abuse for a very long time. If and when disclosure does occur, they tend to minimize the severity of it, hoping to get protection and assistance without revealing the more embarrassing and potentially damaging aspects of their experience. As time passes, they may feel more comfortable relating additional victimization. Unfortunately, the delay, coupled with inconsistency in the accounts of what happened, is often interpreted to be a sign of a lack of veracity.

The child advocate must be aware of these common behaviors and responses in child victims and prevent them from becoming impediments in sexual abuse cases.

> *"As many as a quarter [of doctoral-level psychologists] may harbor beliefs and engage in practices that are questionable."*

MEMORIES OF ABUSE ARE CREATED BY THERAPISTS

Elizabeth Loftus

In recent years, controversy has abounded over the validity of repressed memories of child abuse that have resurfaced in some adults during therapy. In the following viewpoint, Elizabeth Loftus argues that many therapists falsely "diagnose" their patients as incest survivors, regardless of whether the patient has any memories of being abused. Moreover, Loftus asserts, through the use of questionable methods such as guided visualization and hypnosis, therapists can create false memories in their patients. Loftus is a professor of psychology at the University of Washington in Seattle.

As you read, consider the following questions:

1. How does the Ohio psychotherapist mentioned by the author explain the pseudopatient's inability to remember being abused?
2. In Loftus's opinion, how does the Southwestern therapist pursue her "sex-abuse agenda"?
3. What, according to Loftus, is the "one final tragic consequence" of believing in repressed memories?

Reprinted from Elizabeth Loftus, "Remembering Dangerously," *Skeptical Inquirer*, March/April 1995, by permission of the *Skeptical Inquirer*.

We live in a strange and precarious time that resembles at its heart the hysteria and superstitious fervor of the witch trials of the sixteenth and seventeenth centuries. Men and women are being accused, tried, and convicted with no proof or evidence of guilt other than the word of the accuser. Even when the accusations involve numerous perpetrators, inflicting grievous wounds over many years, even decades, the accuser's pointing finger of blame is enough to make believers of judges and juries. Individuals are being imprisoned on the "evidence" provided by memories that come back in dreams and flashbacks—memories that did not exist until a person wandered into therapy and was asked point-blank, "Were you ever sexually abused as a child?" And then begins the process of excavating the "repressed" memories through invasive therapeutic techniques, such as age regression, guided visualization, trance writing, dream work, body work, and hypnosis.

One case that seems to fit the mold led to highly bizarre satanic-abuse memories. An account of the case is described in detail by one of the expert witnesses and is briefly reviewed by Elizabeth Loftus and K. Ketcham.

A woman in her mid-seventies and her recently deceased husband were accused by their two adult daughters of rape, sodomy, forced oral sex, torture by electric shock, and the ritualistic murder of babies. The older daughter, 48 years old at the time of the lawsuit, testified that she was abused from infancy until age 25. The younger daughter alleged abuse from infancy to age 15. A granddaughter also claimed that she was abused by her grandmother from infancy to age 8.

The memories were recovered when the adult daughters went into therapy in 1987 and 1988. After the breakup of her third marriage, the older daughter started psychotherapy, eventually diagnosing herself as a victim of multiple-personality disorder and satanic ritual abuse. She convinced her sister and her niece to begin therapy and joined in their therapy sessions for the first year. The two sisters also attended group therapy with other multiple-personality-disorder patients who claimed to be victims of satanic ritual abuse.

"Remembering" Satanic Ritual Abuse

In therapy the older sister recalled a horrifying incident that occurred when she was four or five years old. Her mother caught a rabbit, chopped off one of its ears, smeared the blood over her body, and then handed the knife to her, expecting her to kill the animal. When she refused, her mother poured scalding water over her arms. When she was 13 and her sister was still in diapers, a group of Satanists demanded that the sisters disembowel a dog with a knife. She remembered being forced to watch as a man who threatened to divulge the secrets of the cult was burned with a torch. Other members of the cult were subjected to electric shocks in rituals that took place in a cave. The cult even made her murder her own newborn baby. When asked for more details about these horrific events, she testified in court that her memory was impaired because she was frequently drugged by the cult members.

The younger sister remembered being molested on a piano bench by her father while his friends watched. She recalled being impregnated by members of the cult at ages 14 and 16, and both pregnancies were ritually aborted. She remembered one incident in the library where she had to eat a jar of pus and another jar of scabs. Her daughter remembered seeing her grandmother in a black robe carrying a candle and being drugged on two occasions and forced to ride in a limousine with several prostitutes.

The jury found the accused woman guilty of neglect. It did not find any intent to harm and thus refused to award monetary damages. Attempts to appeal the decision have failed.

Are the women's memories authentic? The "infancy" memories are almost certainly false memories given the scientific literature on childhood amnesia. Moreover, no evidence in the form of bones or dead bodies was ever produced that might have corroborated the human-sacrifice memories. If these memories are indeed false, as they appear to be, where would they come from? George Ganaway, a clinical assistant professor of psychiatry at the Emory University School of Medicine, has proposed that unwitting suggestions from therapy play an important role in the development of false satanic memories.

WHAT GOES ON IN THERAPY?

Since therapy is done in private, it is not particularly easy to find out what really goes on behind that closed door. But there are clues that can be derived from various sources. Therapists' accounts, patients' accounts, and sworn statements from litigation have revealed that highly suggestive techniques go on in some therapists' offices.

Other evidence of misguided if not reckless beliefs and practices comes from several cases in which private investigators, posing as patients, have gone undercover into therapists' offices. In one case, the pseudopatient visited the therapist complaining about nightmares and trouble sleeping. On the third visit to the therapist, the investigator was told that she was an incest survivor. In another case, Cable News Network sent an employee undercover to the offices of an Ohio psychotherapist (who was supervised by a psychologist) wired with a hidden video camera. The pseudopatient complained of feeling depressed and having recent relationship problems with her husband. In the first session, the therapist diagnosed "incest survivor," telling the pseudopatient she was a "classic case." When the pseudopatient returned for her second session, puzzled about her lack of memory, the therapist told her that her reaction was typical and that she had repressed the memory because the trauma was so awful. A third case, based on surreptitious recordings of a therapist from the Southwestern region of the United States, was inspired by the previous efforts.

INSIDE A SOUTHWESTERN THERAPIST'S OFFICE

In the summer of 1993, a woman (call her "Willa") had a serious problem. Her older sister, a struggling artist, had a dream that she reported to her therapist. The dream got interpreted as evidence of a history of sexual abuse. Ultimately the sister confronted the parents in a videotaped session at the therapist's office. The parents were mortified; the family was wrenched irreparably apart.

Willa tried desperately to find out more about the sister's therapy. On her own initiative, Willa hired a private investigator to pose as a patient and seek therapy from the sister's therapist. The private investigator called herself Ruth. She twice visited the therapist, an M.A. in counseling and guidance who was supervised by a Ph.D., and secretly tape-recorded both of the sessions.

In the first session, Ruth told the therapist that she had been rear-ended in an auto accident a few months earlier and was having trouble getting over it. Ruth said that she would just sit for weeks and cry for no apparent reason. The therapist seemed totally disinterested in getting any history regarding the accident, but instead wanted to talk about Ruth's childhood. While discussing her early life, Ruth volunteered a recurring dream that she had had in childhood and said the dream had now returned. In the dream she is 4 or 5 years old and there is a massive white bull after her that catches her and gores her somewhere in the upper thigh area, leaving her covered with blood.

"GUIDED IMAGERY"

The therapist decided that the stress and sadness that Ruth was currently experiencing was tied to her childhood, since she'd had the same dream as a child. She decided the "night terrors" (as she called them) were evidence that Ruth was suffering from post-traumatic-stress disorder (PTSD). They would use guided imagery to find the source of the childhood trauma. Before actually launching this approach, the therapist informed her patient that she, the therapist, was an incest survivor: "I was incested by my grandfather."

During the guided imagery, Ruth was asked to imagine herself as a little child. She then talked about the trauma of her parents' divorce and of her father's remarriage to a younger woman who resembled Ruth herself. The therapist wanted to know if Ruth's father had had affairs, and she told Ruth that hers had, and that this was a "generational" thing that came from the grandfathers. The therapist led Ruth through confusing/suggestive/manipulative imagery involving a man holding down a little girl somewhere in a bedroom. The therapist decided that Ruth was suffering from a "major grief issue" and told her it was sexual: "I don't think, with the imagery and his marrying someone who looks like you, that it could be anything else."

The second session, two days later, began:

Pseudopatient: You think I am quite possibly a victim of sexual abuse?

Therapist: Um-huh. Quite possibly. It's how I would put it. You know, you don't have the real definitive data that says that, but, um, the first thing that made me think about that was the blood on your thighs. You know, I just wonder, like where would that come from in a child's reality. And, um, the fact that in the imagery the child took you or the child showed you the bedroom and your father holding you down in the bedroom . . . it would be really hard for me to think otherwise. . . . Something would have to come up in your work to really prove that it really wasn't about sexual abuse.

Ruth said she had no memory of such abuse but that didn't dissuade the therapist for a minute.

> Pseudopatient: . . . I can remember a lot of anger and fear associated with him, but I can't recall physical sexual abuse. Do people always remember?

> Therapist: No. . . . Hardly ever. . . . It happened to you a long time ago and your body holds on to the memory and that's why being in something like a car accident might trigger memories. . . .

The therapist shared her own experiences of abuse, now by her father, which supposedly led to anorexia, bulimia, overspending, excessive drinking, and other destructive behaviors from which the therapist had presumably now recovered. For long sections of the tape it was hard to tell who was the patient and who was the therapist.

Later the therapist offered these bits of wisdom:

> I don't know how many people I think are really in psychiatric hospitals who are really just incest survivors or, um, have repressed memories.

> It will be a grief issue that your father was—sexualized you—and was not an appropriate father.

> You need to take that image of yourself as an infant, with the hand over, somebody's trying to stifle your crying, and feeling pain somewhere as a memory.

CONFRONTING THE "PERPETRATOR"

The therapist encouraged Ruth to read two books: The Courage To Heal, which she called the "bible of healing from childhood sexual abuse," and the workbook that goes with it. She made a special point of talking about the section on confrontation with the perpetrator. Confrontation, she said, wasn't necessarily for everyone. Some don't want to do it if it will jeopardize their inheritance, in which case, the therapist said, you can do it after the person is dead—you can do eulogies. But confrontation is empowering, she told Ruth.

Then to Ruth's surprise, the therapist described the recent confrontation she had done with Willa's sister (providing sufficient detail about the unnamed patient that there could be little doubt about who it was).

> Therapist: I just worked with someone who did do it with her parents. Called both of her parents in and we did it in here. . . . Its empowering because you're stepping out on your own. She said she felt like she was 21, and going out on her own for the first time, you know, that's what she felt like. . . .

Pseudopatient: And, did her parents deny or—

Therapist: Oh, they certainly did—

Pseudopatient: Did she remember, that she—she wasn't groping like me?

Therapist: She groped a lot in the beginning. But it sort of, you know, just like pieces of a puzzle, you know, you start to get them and then eventually you can make a picture with it. And she was able to do that. And memory is a funny thing. It's not always really accurate in terms of ages, and times and places and that kind of thing. Like you may have any variable superimposed on another. Like I have a friend who had an ongoing sexual abuse and she would have a memory of, say, being on this couch when she was seven and being abused there, but they didn't have that couch when she was seven, they had it when she was five. . . . It doesn't discount the memory, it just means that it probably went on more than once and so those memories overlap. . . .

Pseudopatient: This woman who did the confrontation, is she free now? Does she feel freed over it?

Therapist: Well, she doesn't feel free from her history . . . but she does feel like she owns it now and it doesn't own her . . . and she has gotten another memory since the confrontation. . . .

CREATING MEMORIES

Ruth tried again to broach the subject of imagination versus memory:

Pseudopatient: How do we know, when the memories come, what are symbols, that it's not our imagination or something?

Therapist: Why would you image this, of all things. If it were your imagination, you'd be imaging how warm and loving he was. . . . I have a therapist friend who says that the only proof she needs to know that something happened is if you think it might have.

At the doorway as Ruth was leaving, her therapist asked if she could hug her, then did so while telling Ruth how brave she was. A few weeks later, Ruth got a bill. She was charged $65 for each session.

Dorothy Rabinowitz put it well: "The beauty of the repressed incest explanation is that, to enjoy its victim benefits, and the distinction of being associated with a survivor group, it isn't even necessary to have any recollection that such abuse took place." Actually, being a victim of abuse without any memories does not sit well, especially when group therapy comes into play and women without memories interact with those who do have memories. The pressure to find memories can be very great.

J.A. Chu pointed out one of the dangers of pursuing a fruitless search (for memories): it masks the real issues from therapeutic exploration. Sometimes patients produce "ever more grotesque and increasingly unbelievable stories in an effort to discredit the material and break the cycle. Unfortunately, some therapists can't take the hint!"

The Southwestern therapist who treated Ruth diagnosed sexual trauma in the first session. She pursued her sex-abuse agenda in the questions she asked, in the answers she interpreted, in the way she discussed dreams, in the books she recommended. An important question remains as to how common these activities might be. Some clinicians would like to believe that the problem of overzealous psychotherapists is on a "very small" scale. A recent survey of doctoral-level psychologists indicates that as many as a quarter may harbor beliefs and engage in practices that are questionable. That these kinds of activities can and do sometimes lead to false memories seems now to be beyond dispute. That these kinds of activities can create false victims, as well as hurt true ones, also seems now to be beyond dispute. . . .

FALSE MEMORY CREATION IS ENDEMIC TO PSYCHOTHERAPY

Many of us would have serious reservations about the kind of therapy practiced by the Southwestern therapist who treated pseudopatient Ruth. Even recovered-memory supporters like John Briere might agree. He did, after all, say quite clearly: "Unfortunately, a number of clients and therapists appear driven to expose and confront every possible traumatic memory." Briere notes that extended and intense effort to make a client uncover all traumatic material is not a good idea since this is often to the detriment of other therapeutic tasks, such as support, consolidation, desensitization, and emotional insight.

Some will argue that the vigorous exploration of buried sex-abuse memories is acceptable because it has been going on for a long time. In fact, to think it is fine to do things the way they've always been done is to have a mind that is as closed and dangerous as a malfunctioning parachute. It is time to recognize that the dangers of false-memory creation are endemic to psychotherapy. T.W. Campbell makes reference to Thomas Kuhn as he argues that the existing paradigm (the theories, methods, procedures) of psychotherapy may no longer be viable. When this happens in other professions, a crisis prevails and the profession must undertake a paradigm shift.

ALTERNATIVES TO REPRESSED MEMORY THERAPY

It may be time for that paradigm shift and for an exploration of new techniques. At the very least, therapists should not let sexual trauma overshadow all other important events in a patient's life. Perhaps there are other explanations for the patient's current symptoms and problems. Good therapists remain open to alternative hypotheses. N.C. Andreasen, for example, urges practitioners to be open to the hypothesis of metabolic or neurochemical abnormalities as cause of a wide range of mental disorders. Even pharmacologically sophisticated psychiatrists sometimes refer their patients to neurologists, endocrinologists, and urologists. For less serious mental problems we may find, as physicians did before the advent of powerful antibiotics, that they are like many infections—self-limiting, running their course and then ending on their own.

When it comes to serious diseases, a question that many people ask of their physicians is "How long have I got?" As R. Buckman and K. Sabbagh have aptly pointed out, this is a difficult question to answer. Patients who get a "statistical" answer often feel angry and frustrated. Yet an uncertain answer is often the truthful answer. When a psychotherapy patient asks, "Why am I depressed?" the therapist who refrains from giving an erroneous answer, however frustrating silence might be, is probably operating closer to the patient's best interests. Likewise, nonconventional "healers" who, relative to conventional physicians, give their patients unwarranted certainty and excess attention, may make the patients temporarily feel better, but in the end may not be helping them at all.

Bad therapy based on bad theory is like a too-heavy oil that, instead of lubricating, can gum up the works—slowing everything down and heating everything up. When the mental works are slowed down and heated up, stray particles of false memory can, unfortunately, get stuck in it. . . .

We live in a culture of accusation. When it comes to molestation, the accused is almost always considered guilty as charged. Some claims of sexual abuse are as believable as any other reports based on memory, but others may not be. However, not all claims are true. As W. Reich has argued: "When we uncritically embrace reports of recovered memories of sexual abuse, and when we nonchalantly assume that they must be as good as our ordinary memories, we debase the coinage of memory altogether." Uncritical acceptance of every single claim of a recovered memory of sexual abuse, no matter how bizarre, is not good for anyone—not the client, not the family, not the mental-health profession, not the precious human faculty of memory. And let us not forget one final tragic consequence of overenthusiastic embracing of every supposedly de-repressed memory; these activities are sure to trivialize the genuine memories of abuse and increase the suffering of real victims who wish and deserve, more than anything else, just to be believed.

> "For victims of childhood sexual abuse, forgetting the abuse is not unusual."

MOST MEMORIES OF ABUSE ARE VALID

Jennifer J. Freyd

Jennifer J. Freyd contends in the following viewpoint that because their experience of sexual abuse is so traumatic, many survivors repress their memories of the abuse or discredit their own recollections. She maintains that it is extremely common for victims of child sexual abuse to forget all or part of the abuse. Moreover, claims Freyd, while some bad therapists may instigate false memories of abuse, most memories of abuse that are recalled in therapy are valid. Freyd is the author of the book *Betrayal Trauma: The Logic of Forgetting Childhood Abuse*, from which the following viewpoint is excerpted.

As you read, consider the following questions:

1. According to Freyd, what percentage of the women in Linda Meyer Williams's study could not remember being sexually abused at some point after the abuse had occurred?
2. Why do survivors of child sexual abuse commonly doubt the reality of their own memories, in the author's opinion?
3. In Freyd's words, why are memories of child sexual abuse often recovered during therapy?

Reprinted, by permission of the publisher, from Jennifer J. Freyd, *Betrayal Trauma*, Cambridge, MA: Harvard University Press, copyright ©1996 by Jennifer J. Freyd. Documentation from the original text has been omitted.

Doubt about whether sexual abuse can be forgotten is at the heart of the current controversy [about recovered memories of child sexual abuse]. Can people forget such things? Despite difficulties with research in this area, a great deal of empirical evidence for forgetting traumatic events has been recorded. Psychogenic amnesia has been documented for a variety of traumatic experiences, including veterans' amnesia for their combat experiences. Bruno Bettelheim described forgetting his experiences in Nazi concentration camps: "Anything that had to do with present hardships was so distressing that one wished to repress it, to forget it. Only what was unrelated to present suffering was emotionally neutral and could hence be remembered."

More recently researchers have documented amnesia for childhood sexual abuse. John Briere and Jon Conte reported results from a large study in which over 59% of adults reporting sexual abuse also reported amnesia for the abuse at some point. Shirley Feldman-Summers and Kenneth Pope reported that approximately 24% of a national sample of psychologists indicated that they had experienced sexual and/or physical abuse in childhood; of those abuse survivors approximately 40% reported a period when they had forgotten some or all of the abuse.

Elizabeth Loftus, Sara Polonsky, and Mindy Fullilove reported that 54% of women in an outpatient substance abuse treatment group reported a history of childhood sexual abuse; of these, 19% reported that they had forgotten the abuse for a period of time and that later the memory returned. An additional 12% reported a period of partial forgetting. Thus 31% of the participants in this study reported some disruption in their memory for the sexual abuse.

The studies by Briere and Conte, Feldman-Summers and Pope, and Loftus, Polonsky, and Fullilove are *retrospective*—that is, adults were asked about their childhood abuse histories and about the persistence of their memory for that abuse. Depending on the form of the question and the population studied, the rates of reported amnesia appear to vary from moderate to high.

WILLIAMS'S STUDY OF AMNESIA FOR CHILDHOOD SEXUAL ABUSE

There is also an important *prospective* study of amnesia for childhood sexual abuse by Linda Meyer Williams. From 1973 through 1975, 206 girls (aged ten months to twelve years) were examined in the hospital emergency room of a major northeastern city as the result of reports of sexual abuse. Then, in 1990 and 1991, 136 of these victims of sexual abuse were located and interviewed. From this group Williams was able to analyze the memories of a subsample of 129 of these women.

Williams compared the women's memories of their childhood experiences with the childhood sexual abuse documented as a result of the hospital admission. The women were eighteen to thirty-one years old at the time of the interviews. They were interviewed privately by a trained interviewer. The typical interview took three hours. The women were asked a series of questions about their experiences with sexual contact during childhood. The interview procedure was designed in such a way that the women might feel comfortable making such disclosures. Forty-nine of these women (38% of the sample) did not report the abuse that had led to their hospital admission as children, nor did they report any other abuse by the same offender.

KEY FINDINGS ABOUT MEMORY AND CHILD SEXUAL ABUSE

Williams anticipated and responded to many questions about her methodology, analyses, and conclusions. In anticipation of the criticism that failure to report is not evidence of failure to recall, she conducted additional analyses to test alternative explanations for her results. For instance, to test the hypothesis that women who did not report the abuse were simply reluctant to talk about very personal matters, she devised a way to measure their willingness to divulge personal information. Those who did not recall the abuse were no less likely to tell the interviewer about confidential or potentially embarrassing information about their sexual history than those who did recall abuse. In separate analyses Williams rejected alternative explanations based on infantile amnesia (although she did find that age was related to amnesia, amnesia rates were still quite high even for the group who were eleven and twelve years old at the time of the abuse) and the possibility that the sexual abuse was simply not significant enough to be remembered. In addition Williams was able to respond to the assertion that sexual abuse was not recalled because it never occurred; she analyzed the 23 cases that met the highest standard for validity and found that for those cases the no-recall rate was even higher (52%) than for the group as a whole.

Williams's study will continue to invite both criticism and acclaim. Replications and extensions of this study are certainly needed, given the import of the findings. In the meantime the data Williams has collected strongly support the claim that women who are sexually abused in childhood do not always remember that abuse as adults.

Williams also investigated recovered memories. She found that of the women who did recall the abuse that was documented in their 1970s records, approximately one in six reported some previous period when they had forgotten it. That is, approximately 10% of her total sample reported recovered memories.

FORGETTING ABUSE IS NOT UNUSUAL

This suggests that close to half of the women in Williams's study—women with documented sexual abuse histories—could not remember the abuse at the time of the interview or some time before that. In other words, this study suggests that for victims of childhood sexual abuse, *forgetting the abuse is not unusual*. Williams suggests that victims of never-discussed, never-documented abuse may be even more likely to forget the abuse than survivors of documented abuse.

When current accounts of the abuse and the records from the 1970s were compared, Williams found that the women with recovered memories had no more discrepancies in their accounts than did those women who reported that they always remembered the abuse. Williams concluded, "Some women, it appears, do reliably recover memories of child sexual abuse." But she also found that the women with recovered memories of documented events tended to be skeptical of their memories, referring to them as possibly just "dreams."

While always remembering a traumatic experience (hypermnesia) and not being able to remember it at all (amnesia) seem at first glance to be mutually exclusive phenomena, in fact the two responses exist simultaneously. Mary Harvey and Judith Herman have suggested that partial amnesia for abuse events accompanied by a mixture of delayed recall and delayed understanding is the most common pattern observed clinically among survivors of childhood sexual abuse. In keeping with this, Laura S. Brown observed that the notion of the "real" trauma survivor "who always remembers gave way to the empirically derived data on actual trauma survivors who suffer from alternating experiences of hypermnesia and amnesia."

RATES OF AMNESIA

Judith Herman and Emily Schatzow investigated the veracity of recovered memories and the persistence of memory of sexual abuse among a group of 53 women who participated in short-term therapy groups for incest survivors. They found that 20 of the patients (38%) had always remembered the abuse, 19 (36%) had moderate memory loss, and 14 (26%) had severe memory loss. The 62% overall amnesia rate in this study was very high; interestingly, the vast majority of women in this group (75%) were abused by their fathers or stepfathers, and abuse by a parent is a primary risk factor for amnesia.

RATES OF FORGETTING SEXUAL ABUSE

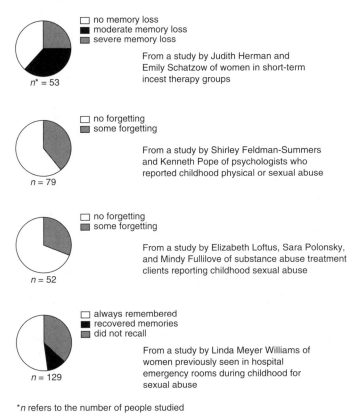

□ no memory loss
■ moderate memory loss
▨ severe memory loss

From a study by Judith Herman and Emily Schatzow of women in short-term incest therapy groups

$n^* = 53$

□ no forgetting
▨ some forgetting

From a study by Shirley Feldman-Summers and Kenneth Pope of psychologists who reported childhood physical or sexual abuse

$n = 79$

□ no forgetting
▨ some forgetting

From a study by Elizabeth Loftus, Sara Polonsky, and Mindy Fullilove of substance abuse treatment clients reporting childhood sexual abuse

$n = 52$

□ always remembered
■ recovered memories
▨ did not recall

From a study by Linda Meyer Williams of women previously seen in hospital emergency rooms during childhood for sexual abuse

$n = 129$

*n refers to the number of people studied

Jennifer J. Freyd, *Betrayal Trauma: The Logic of Forgetting Childhood Abuse*, 1996.

In retrospective studies, we cannot rule out the possibility that those who report always remembering abuse have in fact forgotten some parts of the abuse but did not recover the memories and thus could not report the memory failure. Similarly, we cannot be sure of the accuracy of the memories; it is possible some of the recovered memories are false. Herman and Schatzow reported that 39 patients (74%) were able to obtain confirmation of the sexual abuse from another source. Another five (9%) "reported statements from other family members indicating a strong likelihood that they had also been abused, but did not confirm their suspicions by direct questioning." Six patients (11%) made no attempt to obtain corroborating evidence from other sources, and three (6%) were unable to obtain any corroboration in spite of attempting to do so. There is as yet no agreed-upon definition of corroboration in studies such as this; critics might question the reliability of the corroboration just as they question the reliability of the recovered memories. . . .

SELF-DOUBT ABOUT RECOVERED MEMORIES

A number of issues are tangled within the debate about the accuracy of recovered memories. One tangle concerns the evidentiary status of delayed disclosure and expressed self-doubt about the reality of the disclosures. When adults disclose abuse decades after the events occurred, the disclosures are sometimes met with disbelief because of the delay: *If the abuse happened, why didn't she tell someone about it at the time of the event?* This sort of disbelief is often exacerbated when the adult survivor claims that some or all of her memories for the abuse were only recently recovered: *If the abuse happened, why didn't she remember it for all that time?*

Many survivors convey enormous doubt about the reality of their own abuse memories, whether the memories were continuous or not. As Jody Davies and Mary Frawley describe it:

> Where such memories begin as nonexistent or vague—and only emerge in clear form for the first time during therapy—the patient's confidence in the reliability of such memories is subject to the most intense doubting. This could be expected. Of enormous interest, however, is the fact that, even when patients begin treatment with vivid incest memories, a sense of chronic doubting and questions about the accuracy of these recollections almost inevitably plague the therapeutic process. Chronic doubts about what did and did not happen, along with a persistent inability to trust one's perceptions of reality, are perhaps the most permanent and ultimately damaging long-term effects of childhood sexual abuse. Such doubts make it extremely difficult for the patient to arrive at a point where she can come to believe in her own history. It would be hard to exaggerate the pain an incest survivor feels as she struggles to regain confidence in the working integrity of her own mind or the intense pressure that such doubting induces in the analysts to either confirm or disconfirm the patient's questions about the reality of abuse.

SELF-DOUBT IS COMMON AMONG SURVIVORS

Without special knowledge of the natural response to childhood sexual abuse, it would make sense to infer from this sort of self-doubt that the memories of abuse are not true. In fact, however, this self-doubt about reality is common among abuse survivors. As Linda Meyer Williams noted, even women with documented abuse histories doubt their memories, wondering if they are "just dreams."

Davies and Frawley note that the self-doubt about reality expressed by a sexual abuse survivor is inextricably bound to the nature of the childhood abuse itself. They explain that the "imperative" in childhood for the abuse survivor "to subordinate her own perceptions of reality to those of an overwhelming and invasive other represents one of the most insidiously damaging effects of childhood abuse." This childhood imperative then has implications for the adult survivor's ability to know reality:

> The world of the adult survivor of childhood sexual abuse is a fragmented, discontinuous, and often frightening reality that subsumes a multitude of contradictory experiences, frequently eluding logical cohesion and organization. Caught in the cross currents of partisan perspectives, torn apart by the inability to integrate mutually incompatible experiences of reality, and driven by the opposing needs to both obfuscate actual experience and yet be hypervigilant to the ever-present dangers of repeated abuse, the adult survivor of childhood sexual abuse often feels out of control and crazy.

This evidentiary doubt that often follows delayed disclosures and expressed self-doubt in adult survivors has a parallel in the phenomena of the believability of current child victims of sexual abuse. . . .

CAN THERAPISTS IMPLANT FALSE MEMORIES?

A common theme in popular articles about the contested memory debate is that overzealous and untrained therapists implant memories of sexual abuse into their clients' minds. Although many people recover memories of childhood sexual abuse and other traumas without the intervention of a therapist, it is true that many other people do remember abuse only after initiating psychotherapy. Could these recovered memories in fact be "false memories" implanted by a therapist? If therapists can implant memories through suggestion, does this happen often? Little hard evidence currently exists to aid in answering these questions.

There are several good reasons why real memories of abuse may arise in the context of therapy. Therapy may provide the first opportunity for a person to feel safe enough to remember the abuse; the therapist may be the first person to ask the client about abuse; and the client may have sought therapy because of memories just beginning to emerge, which are causing emotional crisis without explicit understanding of the source of the crisis.

Nonetheless, some therapists may indeed be causing false memories. We do not know how often this may occur. It would seem that the ease of implanting a false memory would vary depending on how closely that memory overlaps actually experienced events. Preliminary support of this hypothesis is provided by Kathy Pezdek. Pezdek attempted to plant false memories of events from childhood that were either familiar (being lost in a shopping mall) or unfamiliar (having an enema). Pezdek found that 3 of the 20 participants "remembered" the false familiar event, but none "remembered" the false unfamiliar event.

THERAPISTS ARE UNFAIRLY CRITICIZED

As a young woman Jill Christman recovered memories of childhood sexual abuse. She remembered this abuse while in therapy with a suggestive and otherwise problematic therapist. During the period in which Christman began to remember abuse she was taking [the antidepressant] Prozac, which had been prescribed by her therapist. The memories came to her in a confusing and inchoate way. She experienced great doubt about them. As the memories came to her, she began to believe that she and another child had been abused *together*. This seems hardly plausible. Yet Christman was able to locate the other victim, who had always remembered the abuse and who confirmed Christman's memories. Despite bizarre circumstances (two children abused together) and memories that were initially doubted, recovered in the context of questionable therapy, Christman found corroboration for the abuse she recovered.

But without the eyewitness corroboration, how many would have believed Christman's memories? Without the corroboration, it would have been tempting to think that the therapist had implanted the memories into the mind of a young woman. In this rare case, the memories were corroborated. Most survivors of childhood sexual abuse receive no corroboration, as there are usually no eyewitnesses other than the single victim and the perpetrator, and the perpetrator usually denies the accusation.

Clients who endure bad therapy may nonetheless come to know the truth of their life; unfortunately, that truth may be discounted because of the poor therapy. Even clients of good therapists may be disbelieved and the therapists criticized simply because some find the outcome of the therapy distasteful or because the therapists are unwilling to pressure their clients to suppress the truth of their own lives.

PERIODICAL BIBLIOGRAPHY

The following articles have been selected to supplement the diverse views presented in this chapter. Addresses are provided for periodicals not indexed in the *Readers' Guide to Periodical Literature*, the *Alternative Press Index*, the *Social Sciences Index*, or the *Index to Legal Periodicals and Books*.

Douglas Besharov	"Why the System Fails Abused Children," *Trial*, March 1997.
Paula L. Boland, Sherry A. Quirk, and Elizabeth F. Loftus	"Repressed Memories," *ABA Journal*, September 1994.
Tiffany Danitz	"Caught in the Trappings of Justice," *Insight*, November 24, 1997. Available from 3600 New York Ave. NE, Washington, DC 20002.
John Fowler	"The Troubling World of Recovered Memory," *World & I*, December 1994. Available from 25 Beacon St., Boston, MA 02108-2803.
Malcolm Gladwell	"From the Mouths of Babes: How Reliable Are Children as Witnesses in Molestation Cases?" *Washington Post National Weekly Edition*, September 11–17, 1995. Available from 1150 15th St. NW, Washington, DC 20071.
Dana Mack	"Child Welfare, Family Destruction," *Headway*, December 1997/January 1998. Available from 13555 Bammel N. Houston, Suite 227, Houston, TX 77066.
Jim Morrison	"You Must Remember This," *George*, December 1996. Available from 1633 Broadway, New York, NY 10019.
Wendy J. Murphy	"Debunking 'False Memory' Myths in Sexual Abuse Cases," *Trial*, November 1997.
Paul Craig Roberts	"Charges of Child Abuse Are Out of Control," *Conservative Chronicle*, January 29, 1997. Available from 9 Second St. NW, Hampton, IA 50441.
Ruth Shalit	"Witch Hunt," *New Republic*, June 19, 1995.
Lloyd K. Stires	"How False Memories Are Created," *Gauntlet*, vol. 2, no. 12, 1996. Available from Dept. B96, 309 Powell Rd., Springfield, PA 19064.

CHAPTER 3

HOW SHOULD THE LEGAL SYSTEM DEAL WITH CHILD MOLESTERS?

CHAPTER PREFACE

In 1994, with his parole hearing set for the following year, Larry Don McQuay, a Texas prison inmate convicted of child molestation, made a chilling statement. Claiming to have molested over two hundred children before being caught, he declared that "without the right treatment, I believe that eventually I will rape, then murder, my victims to keep them from reporting me."

The only treatment McQuay believed would cure him of his desire to molest children was castration. However, the state of Texas denied McQuay's request to be surgically castrated because at the time the state had no law allowing such a procedure.

The case of Larry Don McQuay instigated debate around a central issue regarding child abuse: what to do with sex offenders who appear destined to commit more of the same type of crimes once released from jail. Among the most frequently discussed proposals for how to deal with repeat child molesters is chemical castration. Since Larry Don McQuay made his foreboding statement, five states have passed laws allowing chemical castration.

Chemical castration is a treatment in which sex offenders are injected with Depo-Provera, a drug that reduces sexual drive. Studies done in Europe indicate that chemical castration helps to prevent recidivism: The reoffense rate dropped to 5 percent for offenders undergoing the treatment.

Critics of the new laws, however, argue that the treatment, if imposed against the prisoner's will, constitutes cruel and unusual punishment. According to writer Daniel C. Tsang, "Drugging anyone without his informed consent raises serious constitutional issues; to allow society to do it to prison inmates only raises the question, what or who next?" Moreover, warn opponents, those who support chemical castration laws fail to recognize that many child molesters are motivated by violent impulses, not sexual desires. Chemical castration will do nothing to keep these child molesters from reoffending, critics say.

On the other hand, supporters of chemical castration laws maintain that because the treatment can be stopped at any time, it does not qualify as cruel and unusual punishment. In fact, proponents argue, the treatment actually benefits sex offenders by curing them of destructive desires that control their lives.

Chemical castration is only one method for dealing with sex offenders who prey on children. The following chapter offers several perspectives on what should be done with dangerous repeat child molesters.

| "Offenders can generally be integrated fully into society as normal productive citizens after a period of treatment."

CHILD MOLESTERS CAN BE REHABILITATED

Eric Lotke

Eric Lotke, a research associate at the National Center on Institutions and Alternatives, maintains in the following viewpoint that, contrary to public perception, sex offenders respond positively to psychological treatment. According to Lotke, one study found a 10.9 percent drop in child molester recidivism rates after counseling. Treatment programs would make it possible for most sex offenders to be successfully reintegrated into society, he concludes.

As you read, consider the following questions:

1. What, in Lotke's words, is the prevailing stereotype of the sex offender?
2. In the author's opinion, what is the most important thing to realize about sex offenders?
3. Which type of child molesters respond most positively to treatment, according to Lotke?

Reprinted from Eric Lotke, "Sex Offenders: Does Treatment Work?" *Research Update*, April 1996, by permission of the author and the National Center on Institutions and Alternatives.

If you ask the average citizen to describe a sex offender you will probably get a picture of a drooling violent predator, either retarded or scheming, who rapes and kills women and children for sexual pleasure. If you ask what can be done about these offenders, responses will likely range from castration to electrocution because it is believed nothing less will stop them from offending again in the future.

Such stereotypes do not reflect reality but they do drive criminal justice policy. Sex offenders have become the new bogeymen, used by politicians to intimidate and scare citizens concerned about public safety. Often the claims have more to do with scoring political points than creating a safer society.

This viewpoint attempts to bring some clarity to the issue. Though more research is always helpful and needed, enough is now known to draw some broad conclusions: Treated or untreated, few sex offenders reoffend after being caught. Sex offenders actually reoffend less than other types of offenders, and treatment works to lower reoffense rates.

WHO IS A SEX OFFENDER?

The most important thing to realize about sex offenders is that we do not know who most of them are. Sex crimes tend to be private. Often they involve possession of child pornography or soliciting for prostitution, so there is no "victim" in the traditional sense to register a complaint. The most troubling sex crimes occur behind closed doors, with family members or friends, usually children, who are manipulated or intimidated into silence. Most of these crimes involve fondling or undressing; rarely do they rise to the level of sex acts or intercourse. The perpetrators of most sex crimes are ordinary in most other respects. They are family members, hold jobs, play sports and maintain friendships.

In addition, the majority of sex offenders were themselves victims of sexual molestation. This fact does not excuse their misconduct, but it helps to explain it. Addressing the psychological harm done to offenders in the past may help to reduce the harm they inflict on others in the future, thus preempting intergenerational cycles of abuse.

HOW MANY SEX OFFENDERS ARE THERE?

Because most sex crimes go unreported, it is difficult to determine exactly how many there are. A few observations help to clarify this crucial issue. First, reporting and recording of sex offenses has increased dramatically in recent years. Much of the apparent rise in sex offending is related to increased reporting rather than increased offending.

Second, enforcement is more aggressive and definitions of sex offenses are more expansive than ever before. Conduct that was once tolerated is now criminally prosecuted. This gives the appearance of increased criminal sexual activity when, in fact, the changes are in the official response. More than *eight times* more people were incarcerated for lower grades of sexual assault in 1992 than 1980.

Despite these increases, identified sex offenses are relatively rare. Arrests for rape and other sex offenses constituted 1% of all arrests in 1993. Perpetrators of such crimes constituted 9% of state and federal prison populations in 1992, compared to 22.4% for property offenses and 25.2% for drug offenses.

How Are Sex Offenders Punished?

People convicted of serious sex crimes are usually sentenced to prison. According to the 1992 National Corrections Reporting Program, average prison sentences in state courts were 12.8 years for rape (5 years average time served) and 9.5 years for other kinds of sexual assault (2.5 years average time served). . . . Sentences have gotten longer since the information was collected.

Little or no psychological treatment is available for sex offenders sentenced to prison. Those sentenced to probation are rarely ordered to attend treatment sessions as part of their probation.

How Much Do Sex Offenders Reoffend?

Contrary to popular belief, convicted sex offenders have relatively low rates of recidivism compared to other offenders. On average, untreated sex offenders sentenced to prison have a recidivism rate of 18.5%. In comparison, recidivism rates range around 25% for drug offenses and 30% for violent offenses. Thus, people convicted of sex crimes tend to reoffend less than people convicted of many other types of crime.

The public trial, shame and humiliation of getting caught appears to deter most sex offenders from further misconduct. Sex offenders who have been identified, convicted and punished probably present less of a threat to society than do most other offenders.

Does Treatment Reduce Recidivism?

A popular misconception is that nothing can cure a sex offender. This myth can be traced largely to a paper published by Lita Furby in 1989. Furby's paper, however, focused on the lack of sophisticated, reliable data with which to evaluate treatment regimes. It concluded only that evidence of the effectiveness of psychological treatment was inconclusive. Politicians and the mass media picked up this judgment, often converting it to the claim: "Nothing Works!"

That conclusion, however, is against the general weight of the evidence. Most research shows that sex offenders do indeed respond positively to treatment. A comprehensive analysis by Margaret Alexander of the Oshkosh Correctional Institution found far more studies reporting positive results than otherwise.

TREATED SEX OFFENDERS HAVE LOW RATES OF RECIDIVISM

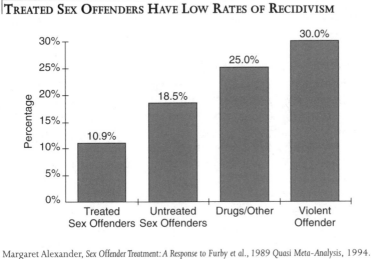

Margaret Alexander, *Sex Offender Treatment: A Response to Furby et al., 1989 Quasi Meta-Analysis*, 1994.

Alexander found that recidivism rates after treatment drop to an average of 10.9%. Thus, a picture has begun to emerge in which treated sex offenders reoffend less than untreated sex offenders. Many sex offenders appreciate the wrongness of their conduct and intensely desire to reform themselves. Treatment helps them to achieve this end.

Moreover, treatment has become more effective as more attention has been devoted to the problem. When Alexander classified the studies by date, she found recidivism rates in recent surveys to be 8.4%.

WHO RESPONDS POSITIVELY TO TREATMENT?

The conclusion that treatment reduces recidivism can be refined further by distinguishing between different kinds of sex offenders. Treatment cuts the recidivism rate among exhibitionists and child molesters by more than half, yet cuts recidivism among rapists by just a few percent. Juveniles respond very positively to treatment, indicating that treating sex offenders as soon as they are identified can prevent an escalation of their pathology. The state of Vermont reports offense rates after treatment as: 19% for rapists, 7% for pedophiles, 3% for incest, and 3% for "hands-off" crimes such as exhibitionism.

One word of caution is in order. Reoffense rates tend to increase over the years and, around the ten year mark, reoffense rates among treated offenders is nearly the same as among untreated offenders. This finding indicates the need for sex offenders to be in booster sessions and maintenance groups for many years. Additional research is needed to produce statistically rigorous and consistent measures of the long-term effects of treatment.

CAN WE AFFORD TREATMENT?

Psychological counseling is expensive, but not as expensive as prison. The average cost of building a new prison cell is about $55,000 and the average cost of operating it for a year is $22,000. A year of intensively supervised probation and treatment may cost between $5,000 and $15,000 per year, depending on the regimen. Thus, a full year of treatment costs far less than an additional year of prison.

Treated offenders can generally be integrated fully into society as normal productive citizens after a period of treatment. Offenders in prison, on the other hand, will continue to cost taxpayers $22,000 a year for as long as they are incarcerated, perhaps even the rest of their lives. Treatment is therefore an essential means of protecting the community at an affordable cost.

THE COMMUNITY RESPONSE

A concerned citizen once asked a criminologist what could be done about child molestation. "Don't molest your children," he replied. The truth behind this response is undeniable. Most sexual misconduct happens within families or among friends; the stalking predator is more a myth than a reality. . . .

The best community response is to focus on recognized ways to keep the problems at a minimum. Punishment and incapacitation have a role to play, but they are inadequate by themselves. Psychological treatment while in prison and after release is vital; education and aftercare are proven to reduce the likelihood of reoffending in the future. Most importantly, the public must make an effort to remain sane and sober in the face of these serious crimes.

"The sexual predation of children is not a crime that can be prevented or controlled by trying to change the perpetrator's pattern of desire."

CHILD MOLESTERS CANNOT BE REHABILITATED

Shari P. Geller

Shari P. Geller, author of the novel *Fatal Convictions*, is a Los Angeles attorney with a specialization in marriage, family, and child counseling. Geller contends in the following viewpoint that sex offenders must be removed from society. The belief that child molesters can be cured, as well as the criminal justice system's failure to adequately punish molesters, has led to a number of rapes and murders of children by repeat sex offenders, she argues. According to Geller, incarceration is the only way to prevent sex offenders from preying on children.

As you read, consider the following questions:

1. According to Geller, how widespread is child sexual abuse?
2. How does Geller characterize the desires of child molesters?
3. What, according to the author, are some of the measures being taken to prevent child molestation?

Reprinted from Shari P. Geller, "Zero Tolerance for Child Molesters," *Los Angeles Times*, December 16, 1996, by permission of the author.

Their names were DeAnn and Alicia and they lived in Fort Lauderdale, Fla. They were sisters, 11 and 7, and now they are dead. Kidnapped, brutalized and murdered in December 1996 by a 30-year-old convicted sex offender who the system—though fully aware of who he was and what he was capable of—thought was better left on the streets.

Unfortunately, DeAnn Emerald Mu'min and Alicia Sybilla Jones are not alone. They are simply the most recent children to die at the hands of a repeat sex offender. They now join Polly Klaas and Megan Kanka, along with too many others to name, all victims of a system that refuses to remove sexual predators from society.

How Many More Victims?

How many more names will be added to the list of victims before we decide we've had enough? How many more times will we turn a blind eye to the startling recidivism rate for child molesters before we say no more? And how much longer will we tolerate misguided judges who refuse to keep sexual predators locked up, instead ordering probation or counseling based on the naive belief that there is a "cure" for what therapists euphemistically call "inappropriate sexual urges"?

The lives and well-being of our children hang in the balance as we struggle to answer these questions. Child sexual abuse is not some fantasy created by scandal-driven media or hysterical mothers. Even the most conservative of statistics, those from sources as reputable as the FBI, are staggering: One in four girls and one in six boys will be a victim of sexual abuse, and 85% of the perpetrators will be someone the child knows. Despite our increased awareness and the call for stiff penalties, fewer than 1 in 20 offenders arrested for sex crimes against children spend any "hard time" in prison. For those who are incarcerated and released, there is a 75% certainty that they will commit new offenses, which may explain why adult sex offenders report an average of 23 child victims.

Sexual Predators Cannot Change

Given these statistics, it is shocking to see how leniently the courts treat this crime and how often child molesters are repeatedly allowed just one more chance. As someone who practiced law for 10 years and who has counseled convicted sex offenders, I know too well that the sexual predation of children is not a crime that can be prevented or controlled by trying to change the perpetrator's pattern of desire. Their desires are immutable and ingrained. Changing the Earth's rotation would seem easier.

The only real answer lies in incarceration. This is not to say that we should ignore the mental health aspects of this problem. To the contrary, those who can be helped should be helped— while they are in prison. And those who can't be helped should remain in prison.

TREATMENT HAS NO EFFECT ON SEX OFFENDERS

A 1992 study of 767 rapists and child molesters in Minnesota found those who completed psychiatric treatment were arrested more often for new sex crimes than those who had not been treated at all. A Canadian survey that tracked released child molesters for 20 years revealed a 43 percent recidivism rate regardless of the therapy. The difference between those simply incarcerated and those subjected to a full range of treatments appears statistically negligible. And the more violent and sadistic the offense, the more likely it is to be repeated.

Andrew Vachss, *New York Times*, January 5, 1993.

The legislature in Washington state tried to create such a system by mandating that repeat sex offenders be psychologically tested before their release to determine if they still posed a risk of harm. If they did, their confinement continued. Unfortunately, the law as worded was ruled unconstitutional. However, in California a similar law withstood in November 1996 its first constitutional challenge in a decision by the state Court of Appeal. The usefulness and necessity of such a law in preventing repeat offenses is manifest and must be pursued in all states.

The same goes for recently enacted sexual predator laws. New Jersey began the first community notification of sex offenders, and now this trend has swept the country. In California, a new law mandates chemical castration for sex offenders after a second conviction, and as an option for a judge after a first conviction (offenders also have the option of surgical castration). In numerous communities, background checks and fingerprints are required for adults seeking to work with children in such organizations as Little League or the Girl Scouts. Such measures have been derided as unduly punitive or hysterical overreactions, but statistical reality suggests that these steps may not go far enough toward safeguarding children against the danger posed by repeat sex offenders.

CHILD MOLESTERS MUST BE INCARCERATED

Still, we have not taken the one step that would provide the ultimate protection for our children: For child molesters, it should be one strike and you're out. Society must have zero tolerance for child molestation. There is something terribly wrong with a system that is incapable of protecting children from a man who:

- for his first offense, attacked a couple on a beach and was only put on probation;
- for his second offense, attempted sexual battery on a 12-year-old girl and was given a short prison term, then let out early due to prison overcrowding;
- for his third offense, sexually battered a 5-year-old girl and was only sentenced to house arrest and probation;
- for his fourth offense (during his period of house arrest and probation on his third offense), was accused of attempted rape on an 11-year-old girl, but never arrested;
- for his fifth offense, kidnapped, sexually assaulted and killed DeAnn and Alicia.

We owe our children better. We obviously can't do any worse.

| *"What could possibly be cruel about a treatment that eliminates the constant urge to molest children?"*

CHILD MOLESTERS SHOULD BE CASTRATED

Michael T. McSpadden

Castration is the most effective means of dealing with sex offenders, Michael T. McSpadden argues in the following viewpoint. He contests what he calls common myths about castration, maintaining that castration is a safe, humane procedure that works to eliminate pedophiles' desire to molest. McSpadden is the presiding judge of the 209th District Court in Harris County, Texas.

As you read, consider the following questions:

1. According to McSpadden, what objections were made to the voluntary castration of child molester Steven Butler?
2. What did the 1989 review of sex offender recidivism conclude about the effectiveness of psychological treatment, according to the author?
3. How does McSpadden respond to the charge that castration is "barbaric treatment"?

Reprinted from Michael T. McSpadden, "Time for Public Debate on Castrating Sex Offenders," *Houston Chronicle*, June 16, 1997, by permission of the author.

Texas Gov. George W. Bush has signed into law a bill allowing repeat sex offenders to seek voluntary surgical castration. The sky has not fallen and the state constitution is still intact. Following California and Montana, Texas has become the third state to take a most important step in finally protecting our children. [On October 1, 1997, similar legislation took effect in the state of Florida.]

An understanding of the events that led to these bills will help dispel the myths and mitigate the scare tactics used by those opposed to castration treatment.

THE CASE OF STEVEN BUTLER

In 1991, Steven Butler was charged in my court with aggravated sexual assault of a child, while already on probation for sexually assaulting another child two years earlier.

I had been quoted in a published report as endorsing castration of sex offenders due to the failure of our criminal justice system to keep them locked up and the failure of conventional counseling in treating them. Aware of the article, Butler asked me, through his attorney, to place him on probation with surgical castration in lieu of prison. He had received counseling that didn't help and was concerned he would continue to rape young girls.

The district attorney's office was notified of the request and talked to the victim's family who gave their approval to the proposed plea bargain. Butler was seen by several psychiatrists and psychologists to assure everyone that he was making an informed and voluntary decision. All parties were confident Butler would benefit from the treatment and would be much less a threat to children in the future.

SCURRILOUS RACIAL CHARGES

A surgeon was contacted who agreed to perform the operation at no cost to the state. It was at this time that local black leaders saw an opportunity for publicity by injecting racial allegations based on the fact that Butler is black and the judge is white. Even the Rev. Jesse Jackson found time to visit Butler in jail.

Because of these racial accusations and the circus atmosphere it promoted, the surgeon withdrew his offer, and Butler was informed we could no longer honor his request. Contrary to several reports, Butler never changed his mind; still, he was deprived of a treatment that would have allowed him to improve his life. He was deprived because black leaders did not want a black man to be the first sex offender to receive surgical castration.

A serious discussion of the effectiveness of this treatment compared to conventional therapy was overshadowed by the scurrilous racial charges which dominated the case.

ANOTHER PEDOPHILE REQUESTS CASTRATION

Immediately after the publicity of the Butler case subsided, I started receiving letters from Larry Don McQuay, a convicted pedophile, asking for information concerning castration and for help in petitioning the state to honor his request for this treatment before his release. For the past five years his desire for castration has been ignored by our state government because it was not "conventional treatment."

Not until his mandatory release to a halfway house in Houston was imminent did the public become informed and our state government finally react.

HOW DOES CHEMICAL CASTRATION WORK?

Treatment ordered for child molesters released from California prisons after a second offense, or after a first offense with a judge's order:

Hormone: Medroxyprogesterone acetate (MPA)

Brand name: Depo Provera

Drug maker: Pharmacia & Upjohn

Dosing instructions: 500 mg weekly intramuscular injections in the arm or buttock

How this drug works: Inhibits the release of hormones in the brain, resulting in a decrease in serum testosterone levels and male sex drive

Possible adverse effects: Weight gain, hypertension, mild lethargy, irregular gallbladder function, testicular atrophy

Wall Street Journal, September 19, 1996.

Unfortunately, it took a self-proclaimed monster like McQuay to again bring the issue of sex-offender treatment to the forefront. His mandatory release finally prompted Attorney General Dan Morales to issue an opinion on the legality of castration.

If castration had been available in 1992, there's a very good chance many sex offenders would have taken advantage of the option before release and countless children would have been spared these heinous crimes.

In discussing the effectiveness of castration it is important to point out the ineffectiveness of conventional therapy and counseling to date. An exhaustive 1989 review of sex offender recidivism in North America and Europe published in the Psychological Bulletin concluded that "there is no evidence that (conventional) treatment effectively reduces sex offense recidivism." To make matters worse, the study showed the rate of reoffending was often higher for conventionally treated offenders than for untreated ones.

Although chemical and surgical castration are equally effective in lowering the testosterone level, the drawback is that chemically castrated men must undergo weekly maintenance injections. Surgical castration enhances public safety by eliminating the possibility that an offender will regain his former aggressive condition.

THE TRUTH ABOUT CASTRATION

The following are some myths and facts concerning castration:

Myth: Castration mutilates a man's body.

Fact: An orchiectomy is a simple surgical procedure in which the testicles are removed via a small incision. The operation is typically an outpatient procedure, and the testicles can be replaced with prostheses.

Myth: Castration is cruel and unusual punishment.

Fact: What could possibly be cruel about a treatment that eliminates the constant urge to molest children? It is unusual only in the sense that it is the one effective and permanent treatment for sex offenders.

Myth: Castration will only make the offender more violent by using other methods to molest.

Fact: Another positive aspect of castration is that is reduces not only the sexual impulse but all aggressive traits in a person, according to studies.

Myth: Castration is a racist punishment.

Fact: Of the 11,000 identified sex offenders in our Texas prisons, 45 percent are white, 24 percent are black and 30 percent are Hispanic.

Myth: The problem is between the ears and not between the thighs.

Fact: This opinion is based on the supposition that rape is all about power, domination and control with no sexual component. The clinical studies show rape involves power, domination and control as well as a strong sexual impulse.

Myth: A civilized society cannot permit this barbaric treatment.

Fact: A civilized society cannot permit the rape of women and children. It has been a long struggle to reach a point where we can have a serious discussion concerning the effectiveness of castration as a treatment.

Until now, we have heard disapproval on castration from a very small percentage of our society—the American Civil Liberties Union, demagogues, sex therapists and their followers.

It is time the silent majority, representing every religion, race and walk of life finally express its outrage to our lawmakers in support of castration for sexual offenders and in support of our children.

> "Requiring castration . . . means we
> have decided it is acceptable to treat
> prisoners as less than human."

CASTRATION IS IMPRACTICAL AND IMMORAL

Atul Gawande

In the following viewpoint, Atul Gawande argues against castration as a suitable punishment for child molesters except in cases in which a violent offender requests the treatment. Gawande contends that laws mandating chemical and surgical castration ignore both the practical and moral dilemmas of implementing this punishment. A medical doctor, Gawande writes a regular column on science and policy for *Slate*, an on-line magazine.

As you read, consider the following questions:

1. According to Gawande, why are chemical castration injections problematic?
2. For what reasons does the author call forced castration immoral?
3. Why do people consider rapists a "special case," according to Gawande?

Reprinted from Atul Gawande, "The Unkindest Cut: The Science and Ethics of Castration," *Slate*, July 11, 1997, by permission of *Slate*.

W ith surprisingly little fanfare, four states have passed laws calling for castration—either chemical or surgical—of sex offenders. In June 1997, prompted by two prisoners who actually *wanted* the treatment, Texas Gov. George Bush signed a law letting judges offer castration as an option for perpetrators of sex crimes. Florida, California, and Montana have all enacted more stringent laws to order involuntary chemical or surgical castration of these criminals.

The technology for castration has evolved considerably, and there is evidence that, in some circumstances, it can dramatically reduce the likelihood a sex offender will strike again. Nonetheless, there are strong reasons that court-ordered castration is a bad idea.

How Can Sex Offenders Be Controlled?

Americans remain frustrated with the inability of the justice system to control rape and child molestation. Dozens of states have enacted so-called Megan's Laws requiring that the public be notified when released sex offenders move in nearby, but people complain that it doesn't help much to know that your neighbor is a pedophile if you can't do anything about it. More states are turning to doctors to solve the problem for them.

Compulsory castration has been used as a punishment for crimes in all cultures dating back thousands of years. In Europe in the Middle Ages, the "eye for an eye" philosophy of *jus talionis* included castration as punishment for adultery or rape. In the 20th century, castration has been practiced in the Netherlands, Germany, Estonia, Iceland, Switzerland, and Scandinavia for rape, pedophilia, and homosexuality. After World War II, its use in Europe was dramatically scaled back, probably because of the increased awareness of humanitarian concerns prompted by the Holocaust.

New Methods of Castration

More recently, research has produced powerful drugs, such as cyproterone and medroxyprogesterone, which reversibly block testosterone production. The drugs' primary use in men is to control prostate cancer, but when injected daily or weekly they reduce testosterone to castration levels. Side effects include serious allergic reactions and the formation of blood clots that can kill patients. The drugs also appear to alter thinking enough to increase suicide rates. The Czech Republic and Germany have reintroduced castration in this modern, seemingly humane form, although only among sex offenders who volunteer for treatment.

Surgical castration is less mutilating than it once was. Orchiectomy, as it is called, is a day-surgery procedure done under local anesthesia. Each testicle is removed through a small scrotal incision similar to the kind made during a vasectomy.

Three of the four new state laws call for sentencing rapists to be castrated, but with some variations. Florida requires judges to impose either injections or orchiectomy for repeat rapists. California does the same, but only for repeat child molesters. Montana allows, but does not require, judges to impose chemical castration on offenders who commit rape or incest after even one offense, if it is particularly heinous.

DOES CASTRATION WORK?

Legislators argue that castration is justified and appropriate, and that by controlling sex offenders' irresistible urges to rape or molest again, the operation allows them to be released without endangering the public. Studies of the European experience suggest they could be right. Of more than 700 Danish sex offenders castrated after multiple convictions, relapse rates dropped from between 17 percent and 50 percent to just 2 percent. A Norwegian study showed the same for selected male and female sex offenders (the women had their ovaries removed). In smaller studies of cyproterone in Scandinavia and Italy, chemical castration was equally effective in some groups of volunteer prisoners, with the most dramatic reductions among pedophiles.

These studies suggest the common argument—that rape is all about power, not sex, and therefore castration won't work—is wrong. Interestingly, a German study found that up to half of the castrated men still could have erections and sex, but their desire was weakened or even extinguished. Over 80 percent no longer masturbated; 70 percent gave up sex. As Fred Berlin, a Johns Hopkins University psychiatrist and expert on treating sex offenders, points out, castration works "mainly in those who are sexually aroused by their crime . . . sadists and pedophiles." Castration takes the impulse away from those with an aberrant sexual orientation, often to their relief.

So what objection could there be to castration of sex offenders? Well, none, if it is carefully applied to the narrow group of repeat sadistic or pedophiliac rapists who accept the treatment. But the court-mandated castration proposed in Florida, California, and Montana raises serious problems.

SERIOUS PROBLEMS WITH CASTRATION

The laws are wrong to apply castration indiscriminately. The studies show that castration is effective in criminals with multiple offenses, especially if they are motivated by sex. But proponents are wrongly using the data to justify mandatory application across the board. In Florida and Montana, all rapists are targeted, even though sadists and pedophiles are only a small percentage of the total. Most rapists appear to be motivated by hatred or anger, not sex. Montana lets judges order castration after just one offense. Dr. Berlin argues that the laws impose "a medical intervention in the absence of evidence that forced treatment is likely . . . to be effective" and make "no effort to medically assess whether [castration] is appropriate for an individual."

MOLESTATION IS MOTIVATED BY VIOLENCE, NOT SEX

Chemical castration assumes that sexual offenders, after losing their sexual drive, will stop molesting children or attacking women. Unfortunately, that simply is not true. Anyone with an elementary knowledge of psychology can tell you that there are many other reasons why offenders commit sex crimes. These are not individuals looking to score on a Saturday night. They are sick, not desperate. Reducing their sexual drive does not necessarily solve the problem. . . .

[Chemical castration laws] reinforce the stereotype that men are sex-crazed individuals and that child molesters and sexual predators need to be drugged to control sexual impulses. In reality, sexual assaults are about violence, power and the humiliation of a survivor or victim.

Larry Helm Spalding, *The Torch: The Quarterly Newsletter of the American Civil Liberties Union of Florida*, August 1997.

Secondly, forced castration is difficult to administer. First, the state must find doctors willing to do the job. (Heaven's Gate members had to go to Mexico for the operation because no California doctor would perform it on them.) California's law suggests letting state workers give the injections without medical supervision, but the serious side effects, and the need to ensure that appropriate doses are given, make this approach foolhardy. It also raises the question of what to do with people who can't take the drug because of the side effects. Would they have to go back to jail? Bringing in released convicts for injections is even more difficult. The longest-lasting drug, medroxyprogesterone, still must be given weekly. Making sure that rapists and pedophiles turn up week after week for an unwanted, potentially lifelong treatment may prove impossible.

Finally, forced castration is immoral. In 1985, the Supreme Court recognized this when it ruled that involuntary surgical castration constituted cruel and unusual punishment. The court may be persuaded to let chemical castration stand because it is theoretically reversible. If this line is crossed, politicians would have little to stop them from seeking forced treatments to control other behaviors, such as adultery (for which castration has historically been a punishment), prostitution, or the consumption of pornography. As medicine's arsenal expands (we already have drugs to limit libido, hunger, and depression), it is conceivable that laws could mandate even wider uses of medicines to control the population.

Many people see rapists as a special case, though, having no objections to extreme measures to stop them from raping again. The crime is so repugnant, they say, that it is hard to treat rapists as people deserving of any concern. Prisoners, after all, give up their rights for having committed such crimes. But as bioethicist Arthur Caplan points out, while "prisoners are excluded from moral life," losing the right to vote, "Americans have not reduced them to non-human status." Unlike Iran, Turkey, or Nazi Germany, the United States accepts prisoners' rights to free speech, legal representation, and health care. We still reject using prisoners for organ transplants or slave labor. Requiring castration for rape means we have decided it is acceptable to treat prisoners as less than human.

| "Detaining and treating [a sexual predator] in a hospital inflicts no unnecessary suffering on him, and it restricts his liberty only as much as needed to protect the innocent."

DETAINING CHILD MOLESTERS INDEFINITELY IS JUST

Stephen Chapman

A recent Kansas law allows courts to confine sexual predators in psychiatric institutions after their prison time has been served. In the following viewpoint, Stephen Chapman maintains that such laws protect society from child molesters and other sexual predators. Moreover, he contends, laws such as the Kansas statute are applied rarely and affect only the most violent offenders. Chapman is a syndicated columnist.

As you read, consider the following questions:
1. In the author's opinion, why are mental institutions the best place for sexual predators?
2. At which child molesters is the Kansas sexual predator law aimed, according to Chapman?
3. Why does Chapman believe that civil commitment is a better choice than longer prison terms for offenders?

Reprinted from Stephen Chapman, "A Surprising Victory over Sexual Predators," *Conservative Chronicle*, July 9, 1997, by permission of Stephen Chapman and Creators Syndicate.

Suppose we are faced with a man who has a disabling disease that can be easily transmitted to children through casual contact. The illness is treatable, but the man refuses treatment. As a result, children unlucky enough to cross paths with him stand a serious risk of inhaling germs that could cause crippling injuries.

What would we do with the man? We could: (a) lock him in prison; (b) let him roam freely infecting other people; or (c) keep him in a medical facility until such time as he no longer poses a danger.

Almost anyone would agree that the only sensible and humane answer is (c). Punishing someone for getting sick would be barbaric. Exposing children to him would be even more indefensible. Detaining and treating him in a hospital inflicts no unnecessary suffering on him, and it restricts his liberty only as much as needed to protect the innocent.

This is all mere common sense, which has been followed in cases of contagious disease for a long time. But common sense is not always abundant in controversies over illnesses that are mental in nature. And that's why the Supreme Court found itself obliged to decide whether a lifelong child molester should be allowed to go free to molest again.

THE CASE OF LEROY HENDRICKS

The case involved Leroy Hendricks, who has been in prison several times for taking various indecent liberties with children. The last time, he was convicted of trying to fondle two adolescent boys and spent nearly 10 years behind bars. But when his term was up, the state of Kansas didn't let him go. Using a new law aimed at sexually violent predators, it went to court to have him committed to a psychiatric institution for as long as he remains a danger, even if he didn't meet the legal definition of "mentally ill." Hendricks sued, claiming the law violated his constitutional rights.

On June 23, 1997, the Supreme Court ruled it didn't. That in itself was something of a surprise, since the court had previously said that a state could not keep a dangerous mental patient confined once he was no longer mentally ill—even though he was still dangerous.

The bigger surprise, though, was that this time, the entire court accepted the notion of using civil commitment as a means to protect innocent people from twisted sex offenders. None of the justices bought the argument of civil liberties advocates that this approach creates a grave threat to individual freedom.

The court's critics were quick to see the sky falling. "The danger is the term 'mental abnormality' could be used to reach all kinds of behavior that may have no relation to mental illness," said Michael Allen of the Bazelton Center for Mental Health Law in Washington. "The law would permit commitment of someone who was just maladjusted."

Allen is not adhering strenuously to the truth. Though Hendricks is not mentally ill in the legal sense, he readily admits to suffering from pedophilia, an undisputed mental disorder. In the past, he has spurned treatment, which he dismisses as "BS," and he insists the only cure for his ailment is death.

Sexual Predator Laws Target Violent Offenders

The Kansas law, despite what Allen suggests, does not allow the authorities to conduct mass dragnets to detain anyone acting morose or wearing a pinwheel hat with a tuxedo. It is aimed only at those "maladjusted" sorts who have committed violent sexual offenses and appear likely to commit more.

Even within this narrow category, the state doesn't have anything resembling carte blanche. Once a sex offender has served his time, the state has to convince a jury beyond a reasonable doubt that he is a sexually violent predator. If the jury agrees, he is sent to a mental hospital—not to a prison. A court is then obligated to review his case at least once a year. If and when the court finds he is no longer mentally abnormal or dangerous, he must be released.

The Principles Behind Sexual Psychopath Statutes

Laws enacted for the purpose of protecting society from sexual predators are nothing new. In the late 1930's, states began enacting what were then termed "sexual psychopath" statutes. In 1937, Michigan became the first state to enact such a statute. Generally, these sexual psychopath statutes allow confinement until full recovery, or until the offender is no longer considered a menace to others. The overriding principles supporting this particular branch of legislation are "(1) to protect society by sequestering the sexual psychopath so long as he remains a menace to others; and (2) to subject him to treatment to the end that he might recover from his psychopathic condition and be rehabilitated."

Mary-Ann R. Burkhart, *Update: A Publication of the National Center for Prosecution of Child Abuse*, Vol. 10, No. 12, 1997.

The state of Kansas has not been using the law indiscriminately: As of June 1997, of 805 sex offenders who have completed their prison terms under the law, only nine have been sent to mental hospitals.

CIVIL COMMITMENT IS A BETTER CHOICE

Civil libertarians act as though they are doing these offenders a favor by sparing them the prospect of institutionalization. But if states were deprived of this option, Northwestern law professor Paul Robinson notes, they would resort to something far less congenial to the inmates: longer prison sentences, including life terms with no chance of parole. Civil commitment offers a better choice that protects society without unjustly punishing offenders who can't control their actions.

In 1995, a Kansas judge took the side of the critics, calling the law "vague, arbitrary and overbroad" and freeing an inmate named Richard Goracke who had been convicted on four different occasions of sexual crimes. Two years later, police were called to investigate the molestation of an 8-year-old girl in New Cambria, Kan. They arrested one Richard Goracke.

> "Once you depart from traditional concepts of crime ... and move into headshrinkery, you can figure out ways to keep anybody you don't like in the slammer forever."

DETAINING CHILD MOLESTERS INDEFINITELY IS UNJUST

Samuel Francis

In the following viewpoint, Samuel Francis challenges the fairness of laws that allow courts to detain violent sex offenders in mental institutions after their prison time has been served. Francis claims that these laws, often referred to as sexual predator statutes, are dangerous in that they give the government power to imprison people indefinitely on the basis of a vague notion of "mental illness." Furthermore, alleges Francis, detaining molesters in mental hospitals does not ensure that society will be protected from them, since sex offenders can be released when psychiatrists consider them cured. Francis is a syndicated columnist.

As you read, consider the following questions:

1. According to Francis, what are the two "dangerous and stupid" features of the Kansas sexual predator law?
2. What reason does the author offer for the popularity of legislation such as the Kansas sexual predator law?
3. What punishment does Francis advocate for sexual predators?

W hat does justice demand be done to people who sexually molest children? There is a wide range of possible answers, from boiling in oil to breaking on the wheel, but these days such penalties are not options. In their place we have psychiatry, and to judge whether headshrinking is more just than older and alternative punishments we have the U.S. Supreme Court.

In December 1996 the Court listened to arguments as to why Kansas's "sexual predators law" ought to be upheld. The Kansas Supreme Court has already struck it down, and while that should have settled the issue, under the federal judge-ocracy in which we live, it doesn't.

There is every reason why a federal court should never have very much to say one way or the other about a state statute, but aside from what is laughingly called "constitutional law" today, there are strong reasons in plain justice why the Kansas law is a stupid and dangerous idea.

WHAT ARE SEXUAL PREDATOR LAWS?

The law provides that "sexual predators" who have served prison terms for their crimes, are diagnosed as having a psychiatrically recognized "mental abnormality or personality disorder" and are likely to repeat their offenses can be confined in a mental institution—indefinitely.

It ought to be obvious what's wrong with the law, but such is the meager condition of criminal justice in this country today that we have reached a point where injustice looks to some people like justice. Some people include more than the citizens of Kansas. Five other states have similar laws, and even more are considering passing them.

A DANGEROUS LAW

There are two dangerous and stupid features of the law. In the first place, it substitutes a mental condition, defined by the head shrink battalions, for a specific act. In the second place, it substitutes indefinite "civil confinement" for specific punishment.

Both concepts are alien to traditional ideas of justice, and there are strong reasons to keep them alien. A mental condition is simply not an act, and no matter how carefully defined and registered in the witch doctors' manuals such a condition might be, it remains far too vague to determine matters like freedom or incarceration.

Who is to say when the mental condition no longer exists and the prisoner (excuse me, patient) can be released? Psychiatrists get to say that—not a judge, not a jury. Who, moreover, is to say what other "mental conditions" beside pedophilia should deliver an otherwise law-abiding citizen to the loony bin forever? And why should we assume that dangerous criminals really will be confined indefinitely? Psychiatrists can release them from padded cells just as easily as soft judges release them from cells of stone and steel.

Who Else Will Be Imprisoned?

Should kleptomaniacs, who feel a compulsion to steal trivial items, be subject to the law? How about "racists"? How about "homophobes," "xenophobes," and all the other pseudo psycho pathologies? It's a good question.

Once you depart from traditional concepts of crime and criminal actions and move into headshrinkery, you can figure out ways to keep anybody you don't like in the slammer forever. Kansas is actually behind the times. The Soviet Union figured it out years ago.

"Mentally Ill" Versus "Mental Abnormality"

Traditional civil commitment law requires a showing, by clear and convincing evidence, that the person to be committed is mentally ill and a danger to self or to others. . . .

The sexually violent predator statute in Kansas applies only to people who have been charged with a sexual offense and convicted, found incompetent to stand trial, or acquitted on grounds of insanity or mental disease. And instead of requiring the state to show that the person is "mentally ill," the Kansas law requires the state to show that the person has a "mental abnormality." . . .

As a substantive matter, the category of "mental abnormality" is a new and broader category than "mental illness." Officials are notoriously prone to overestimate dangerousness, so the sexually violent predator law weakens the most important limit on civil commitment. For example, could a state define illegal drug use as a "mental abnormality" and thereby justify the commitment of any person who fails a urinalysis test for the drugs heroin, cocaine, or marijuana?

Donald A. Dripps, Trial, August 1997.

Laws like this are popular for the simple reason that current criminal law doesn't deal with sexual predators and child molesters adequately. Hence, legislators who want to seem tough on crime and citizens justly angry that perverts are released by the state to commit similar crimes again are all in a pother for throwing away the key.

JUSTICE, NOT PSYCHIATRY

But replacing justice with psychiatry is no more a real solution than replacing justice with repression and terror. The truth is that we have already dispensed with justice in forgetting how to deal with permanently dangerous criminals, so it's not surprising that when we want to deal with them, we resort automatically to injustice.

The proper way to deal with sex criminals and any other kind of criminal is through real justice, which involves designing punishments that fit the crime. Instead of making confinement of predators dependent on psychiatric whim, why not provide for the death penalty for child molesters, or, if that's too tough for the thoroughly modern tough-on-crooks school, life imprisonment with no chance of parole?

PERIODICAL BIBLIOGRAPHY

The following articles have been selected to supplement the diverse views presented in this chapter. Addresses are provided for periodicals not indexed in the *Readers' Guide to Periodical Literature*, the *Alternative Press Index*, the *Social Sciences Index*, or the *Index to Legal Periodicals and Books*.

Mary-Ann R. Burkhart "Sexually Violent Predator Statutes: A New Breed of Civil Commitment," *National Center for Prosecution of Child Abuse*, vol. 10, no. 12, 1997. Available from American Prosecutors Research Institute, 99 Canal Center Plaza, Suite 510, Alexandria, VA 22314.

Donald A. Dripps "Civil Commitment for Convicted Criminals," *Trial*, August 1997.

Don Feder "Life in Prison Isn't Punishment Enough," *Conservative Chronicle*, October 29, 1997. Available from 9 Second St. NW, Hampton, IA 50441.

Gayle M.B. Hanson "Perverts Who Prey on Kids," *Insight*, October 16, 1995. Available from 3600 New York Ave. NE, Washington, DC 20002.

Gayle M.B. Hanson "Serial Sex Offenders: Their Rights vs. Your Life," *Insight*, May 30, 1994.

Gina Kolata "The Many Myths About Sex Offenders," *New York Times*, September 1, 1996.

Larry Don McQuay "The Case for Castration, Part 1," *Washington Monthly*, May 1994.

New York Times "The High Court's Mixed Record Wrong on Sex Offenders," June 25, 1997.

Carl Rowan "Preventive Detention for the Mentally Abnormal," *Liberal Opinion*, December 30, 1996. Available from PO Box 468, Vinton, IA 52349.

Rhonda L. Rundle "Will 'Chemical Castration' Really Work?" *Wall Street Journal*, September 19, 1996.

Craig Turk "Kinder Cut," *New Republic*, August 25, 1997.

Andrew Vachss "Sex Predators Can't Be Saved," *New York Times*, January 5, 1993.

David Van Biema "A Cheap Shot at Pedophilia?" *Time*, September 9, 1996.

Cheryl Wetzstein "The Child Molestation Dilemma," *World & I*, November 1996. Available from 25 Beacon St., Boston, MA 02108-2803.

CHAPTER 4

HOW CAN CHILD ABUSE BE REDUCED?

CHAPTER PREFACE

The citizens of Hamilton Township, New Jersey, were unaware that a convicted sex offender lived in their neighborhood until 1994, when he raped and murdered seven-year-old Megan Kanka. By his own admission, Jesse Timmendequas, a twice-convicted child molester who had recently completed a prison sentence, lured Megan to his nearby home with a promise to show her his new puppy.

Megan's death launched support for community notification legislation, often referred to as Megan's Laws, which require convicted sex offenders to register with the police after their release from jail. Law enforcement officials can then provide communities with information—via computer databases or flyers—regarding the whereabouts of potentially dangerous child molesters. In May 1996, President Bill Clinton signed a federal law requiring state authorities to notify communities of a convicted sex offender's presence.

While Megan's Laws have been lauded by many as an effective way to alert parents to possible dangers to their children, the measures have also drawn criticism. Some critics insist that Megan's Laws constitute double jeopardy—imposing two punishments for the same crime—and therefore violate the constitutional rights of sex offenders. Steve Dasbach, chairman of the Libertarian Party, claims that "either these people are dangerous criminals who should be in prison, or they aren't—in which case they should be released with their full civil rights restored." Critics argue that Megan's Laws infringe on the rights of sex offenders by making it impossible for them to reenter society as productive, law-abiding citizens. As a result of community notification, they maintain, offenders often suffer threats, physical attacks, and even arson from panicked neighbors.

Those in favor of community notification laws, however, argue that children's safety should supersede the rights of convicted sex criminals. As Clinton states, "We respect people's rights, but there is no right greater than a parent's right to raise a child in safety and love." Supporters of Megan's Laws contend that parents have a right to any information that will help them protect their children.

The question of how child molestation and abuse can be reduced is an issue that has generated controversy among legislators and citizens. The following chapter offers perspectives on how the occurrence of child abuse—both within and outside of the family—can be prevented.

| "Communities . . . should know the numbers of children a person has molested and the number of convictions."

COMMUNITY NOTIFICATION LAWS HELP PROTECT CHILDREN

Tere Renteria

Community notification laws, often referred to as "Megan's Laws," grant the public access to information about convicted sex offenders living in their neighborhoods. Many of these laws were prompted by the death of Megan Kanka, a seven-year-old girl who was molested and murdered by a convicted sex offender living next door. In the following viewpoint, Tere Renteria argues that community notification laws help prevent molesters from preying on children. Furthermore, maintains the author, these laws are an important step toward tougher legislation needed to protect children from sexual predators. Renteria is a member of the Solana Beach City Council in San Diego County, California.

As you read, consider the following questions:

1. How does Renteria characterize 90 percent of sexual assault victims?
2. According to the author, to whom should the provisions of Megan's Law apply?
3. Should felons be allowed to return to the communities where their victims live, in Renteria's opinion?

Reprinted from Tere Renteria, "Keep Sex Offenders Away from Children," San Diego Union-Tribune, Opinion section, July 17, 1997, by permission of the author.

A child molestation case in San Diego made me realize how weak our present laws are at protecting our children from molesters.

So-called Megan's laws, under which neighborhoods are notified prior to a convicted sex offender's settling there after serving his time in prison, are the foundation for stronger child-protection laws. However, as I found out, for many children, it is too little, too late.

Persons who molest children are time bombs ticking in our midst. From all indications, there is no treatment that will cure pedophiles of the desire to "hurt" children, yet hundreds of convicted sex offenders have been released from prison in San Diego County to prey again and again.

Because these people are "sick" is no excuse for their actions. They rob our children of happiness and the right to a normal childhood for their own satisfaction.

THE U.S. CONSTITUTION PROTECTS SEX OFFENDERS

The U.S. Constitution presently seems to protect the offenders more than their victims. The argument that "the guilty has a right to get on with his life" is an insult to the children he molests.

Who is rallying for the victims? How can the child whose life has been severely altered "get on with his life"?

Ninety percent of sexual assault victims know the perpetrators. It is a family member, friend or acquaintance. Because of the changes in family and society, more strangers are being introduced to children inside their own homes. There appears to be more danger of child molestation inside the home than from violent sex offenders who steal kids from the street.

UNREPORTED CASES

Too many cases go unreported. It takes very strong parents to pursue criminal charges against a child molester. Even though they are outraged, shame and the fear of subjecting their child to the trauma of a court trial deters them from seeking justice.

Many families hide their dark secret in hope that no one will know. However, without pressing charges, the perpetrator will continue his indecent assault on our children. While the family struggles to forget, the perpetrator is free to prey on more children.

This goes to the heart of our society. Strong legislation that takes away all rights of persons who target children for sexual gratification is necessary.

MEGAN'S LAWS PROTECT CHILDREN

Megan's laws are the first steps in recognizing our need for stronger legislation to protect our children from sexual predators. They are the floor, not the ceiling. We must insist that our legislators "construct" a tougher Megan's law in California.

Those covered under Megan's law provisions should include first-time molesters. Communities also should know the numbers of children a person has molested and the number of convictions. This would send a clear message to all child molesters and improve the safety of our children.

COMMUNITY POLICING REDUCES CRIME

Community notification is best understood as a form of community policing whereby police form an active partnership with the community to reduce crime. This partnership requires effort and intelligence to be successful. Community policing exists on a continuum with a police state on one hand and citizen vigilantism on the other. The tensions toward each extreme must be carefully balanced. Law enforcement officials in Washington have worked diligently to minimize the potential ills of notification, explaining that if the law is abused by citizens, it can be repealed and released sex offenders will once again move to an area without notice.

Roxanne Lieb, *Journal of Interpersonal Violence*, June 1996.

Our children's lives must not be "plea bargained." The sentence must be served. "Commit the crime—do the time!" If sex offenders are released, notification must be made public. Under no circumstance should the felon be allowed to return to the same community where his victims live. . . .

We must all accept the responsibility of protecting our children from sexual predators. If we don't, who will?

| "[Notification] laws create an illusion of safety but do little to prevent [sex] crimes."

COMMUNITY NOTIFICATION LAWS ENCOURAGE VIGILANTISM

Elizabeth Schroeder

In the following viewpoint, Elizabeth Schroeder argues that community notification laws, which grant public access to information regarding the whereabouts of convicted sex offenders, are a simplistic response to the problem of preventing child sexual abuse. She criticizes notification laws for generating hysteria within communities and encouraging acts of vigilantism. Schroeder is an attorney and the associate director of the American Civil Liberties Union of Southern California.

As you read, consider the following questions:

1. In the author's opinion, what problem does community notification fail to address?
2. What, according to Schroeder, is the underlying assumption of notification laws?
3. What does Schroeder suggest might be the unstated purpose of community notification laws?

Reprinted from Elizabeth Schroeder, "Vigilantism Masks Real Threat to Kids," *Los Angeles Times*, Commentary section, January 28, 1997, by permission of the author.

C ontroversy is swirling around a California state law that per-
mits police to notify communities of the presence of convicted sex offenders.

Two cities—one in Orange County and one in Los Angeles
County—have become the first in Southern California to struggle with the ramifications of telling people that a former sex-
offender lives nearby.

In Placentia, a paroled offender was fired from his job, pick-
ets ringed his house and neighbors dialed 911 every time he
left. In South Pasadena, a school passed out fliers with a released
offender's name, address and photograph.

An Overly Simplistic Solution

No one wants a person likely to molest a child living next door.
But legislators have tried to address a serious and complex problem, deviant sexual behavior, with an overly simplistic solution.
Notification laws are an inadequate response to the problem of
sexual offenses against children, which commonly are committed behind closed doors by a family member or friend.

These laws create an illusion of safety but do little to prevent
such crimes. Rather, they encourage vigilantism, which forces
offenders to move from place to place, making them unable to
seek and complete treatment.

Vigilantism

The danger in vigilantism is real. In New Jersey, two men broke
into a house in the middle of the night and beat a man they
mistakenly believed to be a recently paroled sex offender. In
Washington and New Jersey, released convicts' homes were de-
stroyed by arson after their names were broadcast.

Washington, which has had notification laws on the books
for seven years, quickly learned from the arson experience. It
now holds community meetings that include information on
the offender's crime, how to recognize warning signs of abuse
and what measures are being taken to monitor the offender. In
addition, neighbors are strictly warned that harassment is illegal
and will be prosecuted, and that acts of vigilantism could lead to
repeal of the law.

The parolee in South Pasadena had not committed a sex offense in 14 years. He is reported to be suffering from a crippling kidney disease. Not only is he a public scapegoat, but his
parents, who have lived in the community for 20 years, are also
subject to vilification and possible violence.

Unlike other criminals, the sex offender endures a double

punishment. The underlying assumption of the notification law is that, unlike killers, thieves and drug dealers, all sex offenders are incapable of reform. Therefore, after a lengthy prison term, the former sex offender is hounded by a notification law that makes it impossible for him to start a new life.

Darrin Bell, ©1997, Los Angeles Times. Reprinted with permission.

No one advocates that sex offenders be treated lightly. Sentences are stiff, and appropriately so. Judges are already required to consider the facts of the case, the history of the offender and the harm to the victim. They determine whether to sentence him to prison, confine him in a psychiatric facility or make some other appropriate disposition. Judges, like all of us, sometimes make mistakes. Still, the safest approach is to put more and better resources into giving them the information they need to determine the most effective penalty for the individual offender.

But California's sweeping legislation allows police departments unfettered discretion to impose further punishment by alarming residents that a sex offender has moved into their neighborhood.

The Constitution bars punishing a person twice for the same

crime, and federal district courts have struck down community notification in a number of states.

WHAT DO NOTIFICATION LAWS ACCOMPLISH?

We need to ask ourselves what community notification statutes really accomplish. Is their unstated purpose to let the public vent its anger at sex offenders, like a stoning in the Bible? Does the public prefer the illusion of protection rather than admit the reality of sex crimes committed against children?

The real solutions to the real threat include counseling and treatment in prison and after release, establishing neighborhood block watch programs for children and educating parents and children about unwanted sexual advances.

Community notification generates hysteria about a small group of people for a short period of time. It does not solve the problem, but merely moves it—and the offender—to someone else's neighborhood.

"[A parent license] would hold parents responsible for being competent rather than forcing children to endure incompetent parenting."

PARENTAL LICENSURE WOULD REDUCE CHILD ABUSE

Jack C. Westman

Jack C. Westman argues in the following viewpoint for the implementation of parent licensing. Requiring parents to obtain licenses, he maintains, would protect children from poor parenting and child abuse. Westman claims that although most parents would easily meet the licensing criteria, licensing would screen out incompetent parents, which in turn would lead to fewer unwanted and out-of-wedlock births. In addition, the author contends, parental licensure would benefit competent parents by affirming the value of parenthood. Westman is a professor of psychiatry at the University of Wisconsin Medical School in Madison and the author of *Licensing Parents: Can We Prevent Child Abuse and Neglect?*

As you read, consider the following questions:

1. According to Westman, what civil right must be accorded to children?
2. What are the five reasons the author offers for licensing parents?
3. What criteria does Westman propose for parental licensure?

Even though appearing to decrease somewhat recently, violence and crime have reduced public safety in the United States to an unacceptable level. The rising rates of juvenile violence and crime portend greater social problems in the future.

The past focus on socioeconomic, racial, educational, and biological factors that contribute to violence and crime has obscured the most important element—parenting. The main source of these social problems is the cycle of child abuse and neglect that results when parenting fails. Incompetent (defined in legal terms as unfit) parenting is the most important factor in those adult outcomes. Competent parenting protects even biologically vulnerable and socioeconomically disadvantaged children from those outcomes.

A Focus on Preventive Interventions

Because of the high financial and social costs of dealing with adult and juvenile violence and crime, in 1991 the National Commission on Children, appointed by Congress and by the president, urged a change in focus to preventive interventions during early life.

By far most children who live in poverty, who come from broken homes, who receive welfare, who have been abused, or who have criminal relatives do not become habitual criminals or welfare dependent. When any of these factors converge with parental abuse and neglect, however, one of two or three of these children is destined for criminality or welfare dependency. Some are handicapped by brain damage resulting from maternal drug abuse and alcoholism and inadequate prenatal care. All do not learn from their parents the values and personal skills necessary for effective education and for productive employment. These dangerous and dependent persons are increasing in numbers to further drain public funds and to erode the productivity of our workforce. . . .

Society Depends Upon Competent Parenting

Parenting is vital to the future of our society, as the National Council of Juvenile and Family Court Judges pointed out:

> Society must engender within its citizens the awareness of what it is to be a good parent. No public or private agency, child care giver, social worker, teacher, or friend can replace the parent in the child's mind. To the extent that family life is damaged or failing, our children, their children, and the nation will suffer. The high calling of "parenthood" must be more adequately recognized, respected and honored by our society. Therein lies the future of our nation.

Although they are only a small fraction of all parents, incompetent parents gravely endanger our society. I estimate that 4 percent of parents in the United States are grossly incompetent and that 3.6 million of our young people have been damaged by both neglect and abuse. Some seven million have been abused or neglected. . . .

A New Paradigm for Parenting

If our society is to appropriately value parenthood, a new paradigm for parenting is needed. The existing paradigm is that children are the property of their biological parents. Anyone who conceives and gives birth to a child has the full care and custody of that child until the child is damaged by abuse or neglect. No one asks if that person is capable of parenting that child. That person, often referred to as the "real" parent, can lay claim to the child years after the child has bonded to parents who reared the child.

The vast majority of biological parents are in the best position to represent the interests of their children, but we need to move beyond the view of children as the property of their biological parents. A strong argument can be made that every male and every female has the biological right to conceive a child, and that every female has the biological right to give birth to a child. But true parenthood is defined by the earned relationship between parent and child over time. It is not permanently endowed by the events of conceiving or giving birth to a child. We need a new paradigm in which parenthood is a privilege, as it is now for adoptive and foster parents, rather than a biological right. We need to see parenting through the eyes of children and of society.

The Civil Right to Competent Parenting

For the well-being of our society, we also need to accord children a civil right expected by adults: the opportunity to be free of insurmountable obstacles to developing one's potential in life. The civil right to competent parenting is widely acknowledged in declarations of the rights of children in the United States and by the United Nations. Competent parenting is a legal right because incompetent parenting is a cause for state intervention and the possible termination of parental rights. It is a divine obligation when parenthood is viewed as a covenant with God.

A new paradigm in which parenthood is an earned privilege and competent parenting is our objective for all children would focus on preparing young people for parenthood. It would call for nurturant homes and adequate education for all children. It would encourage recognizing the financial value of competent parenting in taxation policies and in the workplace. It would target our resources on identifying, remediating, and replacing incompetent parenting when necessary. . . .

THE NEED FOR PARENTING STANDARDS

The most important, but unrecognized, issue facing our society today is whether or not we value children and the future of our nation enough to try to ensure that every child receives competent parenting. We cannot universally assume competence in parenting any more than we can universally assume competence in any other activity that affects other people. Irresponsible people do conceive and bear children. We cannot rely upon every irresponsible person becoming responsible through persuasion, education, or treatment. Our children and society need protection from incompetent parents who are handicapping the next generation now.

Most adults and teenagers already know that parenting is an important responsibility. For most of the others persuasion and education are sufficient to convince them that it is. But for a small but crucial percentage, the only available means of inducing them to function as responsible parents is by enforcing child-abuse and neglect laws *after* they have damaged their children. But children need society's protection *before* they have been damaged.

Persuasion and education in themselves are insufficient to ensure general compliance with any social value, as is evident in the need for laws against criminal and exploitative sexual behavior. Just as aggressive and sexual behavior can adversely affect others, incompetent parenting also adversely affects others—the children first and society later.

Because our society must contend with the social repercussions of incompetent parenting, government has a role in preventing child neglect and abuse. This could be done by setting standards for parenting in the same way that we set standards for everything else we do that affects other persons—and children are persons. . . .

REASONS FOR LICENSING PARENTS

The time has come to consider protecting children from incompetent parenting by setting parenting standards through licensing before they are damaged by abuse and neglect for five reasons.

The first is the human rights principle that all persons, including children, should be free from abuse, oppression, and rejection. Now millions of children are abused, oppressed, and rejected by incompetent parents. Little is done before these children are damaged.

The second is the civil rights principle that all persons should have equal access to opportunities to develop their potentials in life, an especially important right for children whose future opportunities can be permanently foreclosed by parental abuse and neglect.

The third is the common good principle through which government can regulate activities that are potentially harmful to others and to society. As it is now, incompetent parents harm their children and gravely endanger the internal security and productivity of our nation.

The fourth is the humanistic principle that the future success of children as citizens and as parents depends upon forming affectionate attachment bonds with their own parents. Incompetent parents do not form healthy attachment bonds with their children and thereby deprive their children of learning how to become responsible citizens and parents.

The fifth is that adolescents are not ready for parenthood in modern society after the attainment of biological puberty, a fact recognized by separate rites of puberty and adulthood in aboriginal cultures. Parenthood consists of more than child care. It is a responsible developmental stage in the life cycle that follows childhood and adolescence.

DEMONSTRATING THE VALUE OF PARENTHOOD

A licensing process for parents would demonstrate that our society values competent parenting. It would implement the rhetoric that children have a civil right to competent parenting. It would accord parenthood the status of a privilege rather than a biological right. It would elevate child-rearing from the realm of caprice, accident, and ulterior motives by according parenthood the dignity and legitimacy it deserves. It would encourage people to become more responsible in their sexual behavior and in child-rearing.

A parent license would validate parental rights and focus public policies on supporting competent parenting and on remedying or replacing incompetent parenting. It would hold parents responsible for being competent rather than forcing children to endure incompetent parenting until they show publicly recognized signs of damage. The responsibility would fall on parents to demonstrate their competence before a child is damaged rather than on the state to prove unfitness after a child has been damaged, as is the case now. Parents indeed would bear the responsibility for rearing their children. Then there would be little need for governmental interventions.

Parent licensing would not attempt to distinguish between "good" and "less good" parenting or to prescribe parenting styles. It would exclude only those who are obviously unqualified. It would not be a birth control measure, although it probably would influence procreation by conveying the message that society holds expectations for child-rearing.

PROCEDURES FOR LICENSING PARENTS

The purpose of licensing would be to accord parenting appropriate status in society, not to create a new bureaucracy. As a preventive extension of the child-protective system, the licensing process would be a screening device rather than a definitive evaluation. Establishing procedures for licensing parents would entail little more administrative structure than currently is involved in marriage licensing, birth registration, and protective services for children.

The practical aspects of licensing parents would include its eligibility criteria, its administration, the consequences of denial of licensure, and the question of testing for parental competence.

CRITERIA FOR LICENSURE

The criteria for obtaining a parenting license would fit a straightforward credentialing process, like marriage licensing. Unlike the marriage license, it would be obtained for each parent and validated for each child.

The first criterion would be the attainment of adulthood based on the principle that a parent should be able to be responsible for one's own life before assuming responsibility for a child's life. Eighteen would be a reasonable age based on physical, social, and emotional maturity and the likelihood that the applicant had completed a high school education. For parents under the age of eighteen who still need parenting themselves, parental assumption of responsibility for the minor and the child as licensed foster parents would be required so that the minor could obtain a provisional license that would be fully validated when the minor becomes an adult.

The second criterion would be a pledge by the parent to care for and nurture the child and to refrain from abusing and neglecting the child. If this commitment was broken at a later time, the intervention upon a parent's rights would be based on the failure of that parent to fulfill a contractual commitment to the child with revocation of a license rather than on a quasi-criminal action, as is now the case.

The third criterion would be possession of basic knowledge of child-rearing, such as by completing a parenting course in a school or clinic or its equivalent. In all likelihood, parent licensing would stimulate the development of family life education, already offered in many communities. The mass impact of such a program would likely discourage premature marriages and reinforce awareness of the gravity of child-rearing responsibilities. From the point of view of the educational curriculum, preparation for parenthood is more important than any other academic subject. Moreover, the need for education in parenting is widely perceived today by most parents. . . .

OBJECTIONS TO PARENT LICENSING

No reasonable person would deny that children should be competently parented. Yet any effort to ensure that children have competent parents meets strident objections. Licensing parents seems especially unthinkable to many people.

The intense emotions evoked by the idea of licensing parents often leads to the categorical dismissal of setting any standards for parenting. Underneath these sentiments lie the presumption that children are the property of their biological parents and the mistrust of government.

RESTRICTING INDIVIDUAL FREEDOM?

The political Left fears that parent licensing would unduly restrict individual freedom and could be used as an excuse to curtail governmental support of families and as a tool of racism. The political Right regards parent licensing as an intrusion of government into the private affairs of families and as a violation of the sacred parent-child relationship. Parent licensing actually would identify foundering parents and target private and public programs to help them. It would no more invade the privacy of families than do existing child-abuse and neglect laws. It would formally consecrate parenting.

Setting standards for parenting also can be construed as "blaming" parents who already are stressed by living in an unsupportive society. All parents have acted in ways that fall short of their parenting ideals. The mere mention of parental incompetence in itself can evoke the fear that a parent would not qualify as competent. But a statement by society that parenting is important enough to license would have the opposite effect. Because only a small fraction of parents would not meet the standards of minimal competence, the vast majority of parents would be affirmed. Rather than being taken for granted as a secondary role in our society, parenting would be valued as an essential social institution. The due process of law and appeal procedures would ensure that a competent parent would not be improperly denied a license.

INCONVENIENCE SHOULD NOT BE A DETERRENT

The argument is advanced that we should not inconvenience all parents by a licensing process for which only a small percentage of parents would not qualify. This does not deter us from other licensing procedures that only screen out a similar small percentage of all who apply. In addition, the purpose of licensing parents would be not only to identify vulnerable parents but to generally enhance the status of parenting.

UNLICENSED PARENTS SHOULD LOSE THEIR CHILDREN

Providing healthy and successful rearing environments for the millions of American children now being incompetently reared will be very expensive. . . .

The only long-term solution, I believe, is Jack Westman's proposal that we require prospective parents to meet the same minimum requirements that we now expect of couples hoping to adopt a baby: a mature man and woman sufficiently committed to parenthood to be married to each other, who are self-supporting and neither criminal nor actively psychotic. . . . The only sanction proposed for unlicensed parents who produce a child is periodic visits by child-protection caseworkers who will do an annual audit of each child's physical, social, and educational progress. . . . [The next step] should be to take custody of babies born to unlicensed mothers, before bonding occurs, and to place them for adoption or permanent care by professionally trained and supervised foster parents. The result should be a society in which all children are reared by an adult couple, self-supporting and socialized themselves, and thus— unlike millions of American babies today—with a real chance to achieve the American birthright of life, liberty, and the pursuit of happiness.

David T. Lykken, *Society*, November/December 1996.

Even those who agree that standards should be set for parenting might feel that such a procedure is utopian and unworkable because of the complexities of administering a licensing process. They point to the practical problems involved in predicting parental incompetence and in realigning and expanding protective services in order to deal with the current overwhelming burdens imposed by abusive and neglectful parents. They should be reassured by the screening intent of a credentialing process. They could add their support to allocating more resources to deal with the current situation.

All of the objections to licensing parents can be regarded as insurmountable obstacles, or they can be seen as hurdles to be taken into account in designing and implementing licensing procedures. A process for licensing parents should not be ruled out simply because it has not been done before or because it would be too much trouble. The excuse that according parenting the status of operating a motor vehicle would be too difficult constitutes societal neglect of our children. . . .

PARENTING AS A PRIVILEGE, NOT A RIGHT

Competent parenting is essential for the survival of our society. Parents are in the best position to represent the interests of their children. But because of the damage that incompetent parents cause their children and society, the accountability of parents to society needs to be made clear. This could be done by recognizing parenting as a privilege supported by society, rather than as a biological right, and by affirming every child's civil right to competent parenting.

The ineffective expenditure of our limited resources on trying to repair children and adults who have been damaged by incompetent parenting makes setting standards for parenting necessary today. Setting minimum standards for parenting would help to prevent child neglect and abuse. We should not continue to wait until parents damage their children by neglect and abuse and then apply parenting standards, as we do now.

Licensing parents would lay the foundation for dramatically reducing the need for costly and ineffective governmental welfare and correctional programs. It would affirm parental responsibility for child-rearing and reduce the need for governmental involvement in families. It would increase the general level of competent parenting and positively affect generations to come.

Imagine what our nation would be like if every child had competent parenting. This is not an unrealistic goal if we really care about our future.

> "All of the proposals of parental licensure would eventually encompass all American families, and the predictable abuses would ensue."

PARENTAL LICENSURE IS DANGEROUS

William Norman Grigg

In the following viewpoint, William Norman Grigg asserts that the proposal to require licenses for parents is absurd and dangerous. Grigg maintains that the licensing of parents is a totalitarian scheme aimed at preventing the poor from reproducing. Furthermore, he claims, parental licensure would limit civil freedoms and give the government more control over families. Grigg is a senior editor at the *New American*, a biweekly conservative magazine.

As you read, consider the following questions:

1. What does the author cite as the proposed consequences for unlicensed parents who have children?
2. What are some of the potential abuses of parental licensure, according to Grigg?
3. In the author's opinion, how do proponents of parental licensure justify the assumption of unconstitutional powers?

Reprinted from William Norman Grigg, "Are You Fit to Be a Parent?" *The New American*, January 23, 1995, by permission of *The New American*.

Through the alchemy of controlled media debate, the custodians of respectable opinion transmute the unthinkable into the inevitable. This process appears to be well underway regarding the totalitarian proposal that parents be required to obtain a license from the government in order to raise their own children. Since November 1994, when Dr. Jack C. Westman of the University of Wisconsin-Madison published his book *Licensing Parents: Can We Prevent Child Abuse and Neglect?*, at least two more self-appointed "experts" have ventilated similar proposals, and Dr. Westman has availed himself of high-profile media appearances to promote his scheme.

According to the December 21, 1994, *Dayton (Ohio) Daily News*, noted child psychiatrist Foster Cline has also embraced the notion that "licensing parents is . . . an answer to the youth violence occurring in the world today." Cline is director of the Colorado-based Evergreen Consultants in Human Behavior and was an early advocate of "rage-reduction therapy," a process in which (according to the *Daily News*) children are "forced to deal with their rage and anger." Speaking at the Midwest Children's Conference at Sinclair Community College in Dayton, Cline declared, "Some parents aren't fit to be parents. If you can't pass the sixth grade, you shouldn't be able to have children." Like Westman, Cline believes that parental licensure would provide preemptive protection from crime and other social ills.

Similar arguments have been proffered by David Lykken, a professor of psychology at the University of Minnesota. In his book, *The American Crime Factory: How It Works and How to Slow It Down*, Lykken endorses a system of parental licensure. Furthermore, Lykken targets his proposals squarely at the underclass and sketches detailed enforcement mechanisms and sanctions for those who fail to comply.

As summarized by the Minneapolis *Star-Tribune*, "Under Lykken's system, if children were born to unlicensed parents, the state would intervene immediately. Licenses would be checked in hospital maternity wards. Unlicensed parents would lose their children permanently. Adoptions would be final and irreversible." Furthermore, sanctions would extend beyond the abduction of "unauthorized" children. Lykken informed the *Star-Tribune*, "Repeat offenders might be required to submit to an implant of Norplant [a surgically implanted contraceptive] as a way to keep them from having another baby for five years."

STATE-SUPERVISED ORPHANAGES

Lykken points out that the task of caring for children seized from unlicensed parents would require the development of "alternative parenting mechanisms"; significantly, he believes that this leads us "back to Newt Gingrich's orphanages." Lykken apparently believes that a system of state-supervised orphanages might be established to replace the nation's foster care system: "The foster-care system in most of the United States is very inadequate. I think we should professionalize [i.e., publicly fund] foster care."

Although there are literally millions of generous, decent foster families in this country, the system is indeed a serious problem. Many parents who have been falsely accused of child abuse have seen their children kidnaped by "child protection" workers and placed into the foster care system, only to find that their children have suffered genuine child abuse at the hands of inept or corrupt foster parents. Others, like the Jim Wade family in San Diego, have seen their children taken into "protective" custody and placed into foster homes on a fast track for irreversible adoption. In the Wade case, the child "protection" agency was seeking to have the child adopted before the father could be exonerated of sexual molestation charges. Abuses of this sort happen frequently in the foster care system precisely because of the "professional" elements of that system whose powers would be augmented under Lykken's proposal.

Targeting the Underclass

Dr. Westman has stated that his parental licensure program would begin with homes which receive public assistance. Lykken is even more emphatic on this point: "If you live in the projects on welfare, then you can't have a baby. And that sounds awful. . . . But the question is, if you live in a plague area, have you a right to bring a child into a plague area?" Such statements raise the suspicion that a third "k" is missing from Lykken's name.

However, he takes care to specify that his proposal would eventually apply to all parents, without regard to race or class: "This is not racially based. The facts are, most of the parents who neglect and abuse their children are Caucasian. And from the socio-economic point of view, it is not classist because half of the children who are neglected and abused do not receive public assistance."

Predictable Abuses of Parental Licensure

Should the present welfare system evolve into what Richard Herrnstein and Charles Murray call, in The Bell Curve, the "custodial state," adoption of a parental licensure system like that envisioned by Lykken would be a logical step. Middle-class Americans might even be tempted to embrace such a system as a rational alternative to subsidized bastardy and the incubation of social pathologies in the ghetto. However, in the "custodial state" this question would remain: Who will guard the guardians?

Destroying the Family's Independence

Diagnosing the family as critically ill, those . . . who would license parents are advocating force feeding it a powerful poison in hopes that if it survives it will somehow return to what they consider to be its formerly healthy and functional condition.

To give the state licensing power over parents, however, is only a short step away from giving the state control over all aspects of family life, which would effectively destroy the family's independence and its place as the most important intermediate institution left separating the individual from the full power of the state.

Howard G. Schneiderman, *Society*, November/December 1996.

Although this system would begin with the underclass, all of the proposals of parental licensure would eventually encompass all American families, and the predictable abuses would ensue. For instance: If, as Foster Cline asserts, a sixth grade education is a necessary prerequisite for parenthood, why couldn't the state make graduation from a government-operated high school a condition of receiving a parent license? If, as Lykken suggests, the state could require implantation of Norplant to prevent "unauthorized" births, could it not also require irreversible sterilization, or even abortion? Furthermore, Lykken's suggestion that state officials prowl maternity wards to deter the birth of "unauthorized" children would not be novel to refugees from Communist China.

Avoiding Constitutional Questions

Media discussions of parental licensure have carefully avoided an examination of constitutional questions, clinging instead to matters of "practicality." Implicit in such discussions is the notion that the state has the power to impose such a system should it become "necessary," and licensure advocates insist that "incompetent parenting" has created a social crisis. Westman notes that "the U.S. Advisory Committee on Child Abuse and Neglect in 1992 declared child abuse and neglect a national emergency, and nobody paid any attention to it." Lykken strikes a similar note, declaring, "The 'American crime factory' is turning out these sociopaths at an ever-increasing rate. We can't keep building more and more prisons. We've got to do something to turn off the spigot."

To persuade the public of the necessity of parental licensing, Westman, Lykken, and other advocates are pursuing a version of what could be called the "Burning Reichstag Gambit." Just as the National Socialists stampeded the German public into a police state by screaming, "The Reichstag's burning—suspend the constitution!" advocates of parental licensing maintain that the social emergency created by "incompetent parenting" justifies the assumption of unconstitutional powers by the government. In doing this, they appear to be following a script which was composed during the last decade. . . .

Usurping Parental Rights

In a seminal 1980 essay on the subject, entitled simply "Licensing Parents," philosophy professor and *soi-disant* children's advocate Hugh LaFollette contended that licensing parents is proper because "any activity that is potentially harmful to others and requires certain demonstrated competence for its safe performance . . . is subject to regulation. . . ." According to LaFollette, "since some people hold unacceptable views about what is best for children . . . people do not automatically have rights to rear children just because they will rear them in a way they deem appropriate." Among the "unacceptable views" to be eradicated through parental licensing is the belief that "parents, particularly biological parents . . . have natural sovereignty over their children." From LaFollette's perspective, "to protect [children] from maltreatment, this attitude toward children must be dislodged."

LaFollette is typical of "children's rights" advocates who assume that all parents are potential criminals. Predictably, his essay attracted the attention of other activists who believe that all citizens are potential criminals, and that the fight against crime will require that the state absorb the functions of the home. Criminologist Gene Stephens of the University of South Carolina, who serves as a chapter coordinator for the World Future Society, endorsed the parental licensing concept in "Crime in the Year 2000," an essay published in the April 1981 issue of *The Futurist* magazine. Stephens predicted, "Parental care in the year 2000 may be different from today's and better, *since by then the movement to license or certify parents may be well under way*" (emphasis added).

Not content with the usurpation of parental authority, Stephens suggested a fully-realized program of eugenics:

In most cases, certified couples would be allowed to have their own natural children. In some instances, however, genetic scanning may find that some women and men can produce "super" babies but are not well suited to rear them. These couples will be licensed to breed, but will give up their children to other people licensed to rear them. The couple who raises the child will be especially suited to provide love and compassion and the best possible care that the child feels wanted and needed in society. The very fact that children will feel wanted could lead to better development of their egos and, thus, of their capabilities. Child breeding and rearing, then, may be considered too important to be left to chance. . . . [Wanted] children will have fewer environmental reasons to turn to crime and controlled breeding will result in fewer biological reasons for crime.

"WE'RE ALL CRIMINALS"

Stephens does not appear to be uncomfortable with the totalitarian nature of his proposals. He told The New American, "In China, the government requires parents to obtain a license before they are permitted to have a second child. Unfortunately, when my article was published [1981], our relationship with China was poor, and people would object that 'oh, that idea's just like the communist Chinese program.'" Furthermore, according to Stephens, regarding crime, "It's not a question of us versus them; it's us—we're all criminals." This is because "of the way in which people are socialized in this country. The rite of passage for an adolescent is to break the law, or defy authority. As the [1994] election shows, we don't like government, we don't like authority, and we don't like being told what to do." (Of course, in the American constitutional tradition, the state does not exist to tell citizens "what to do," but rather to protect their individual rights and property.)

Stephens told The New American that although he doesn't think a full-fledged program of parental licensure is an immediate possibility, "a lot of school districts offer—and some districts require—enrollment in Parent Effectiveness Training courses beginning in the sixth grade." He also cites "conflict resolution" programs "which are taught on a mentoring basis or using a peer approach, in which high school students are taught the skills and then they teach junior high kids, and so on." According to Stephens, "there's just gobs of these types of programs in school districts across the country."

THE PARENTAL RIGHTS AMENDMENT

With "experts" emerging to endorse parental licensure, and with preliminary programs like those described by Stephens proliferating through the government school system, traditionalist parents might wish to examine the merits of a proposed Parental Rights Amendment (PRA), which could be adopted at the state level. Of the People, a grassroots pro-family group based in Arlington, Virginia, has created the following model PRA: "The right of parents to direct the upbringing and education of their children shall not be infringed." The legislatures of nine states considered proposed PRAs in 1994, and 12 states—Alabama, Arizona, Colorado, Illinois, Kentucky, Michigan, Mississippi, Missouri, Oregon, Virginia, Washington, and Wisconsin—debated the proposal in 1995.

The addition of a PRA to a state constitution would provide a significant obstacle to social engineers such as Westman and Lykken—a fact not lost upon the child "protection" bureaucracy. When a PRA-style measure was proposed in Kansas, its opponents cynically labeled it the "David Koresh Amendment." State Representative Denise Everhart, an opponent of the measure, declared that "I have a thousand stories of child abuse that I will recite on the House floor one at a time if I have to in order to keep this amendment from passing." Jim McDavitt, director of the Kansas Education Watch network, reports that LaFollette's essay "Licensing Parents" was cited by a critic of the measure during testimony before the legislature's judiciary committee.

The 1994 electoral rebuke of Clintonism may deflect some of the more grandiose social engineering schemes at the federal level. However, the states are planted thick with social engineers like Westman and Lykken who will implement their schemes if they are permitted to, creating precedents which will set the parameters of future federal policies.

> "Instead of assuming children will be better off without parents who have maltreated them, practitioners must ask what it will take to keep the child safe and protect the child from the loss of her family."

FAMILY PRESERVATION PROGRAMS HELP CHILDREN

Margaret Beyer

Family preservation programs attempt to keep families together after incidents of child abuse instead of placing children in foster homes. In the following viewpoint, Margaret Beyer contends that family preservation is a humane and effective approach to eradicating intrafamilial child abuse. Moreover, she argues that when correctly implemented, family preservation programs give parents the resources to develop healthy relationships with their children. A psychologist, Beyer works with children and families and provides clinical supervision in public and private agencies. She also serves as an expert in class action litigation and as a consultant for child welfare reform in a number of states.

As you read, consider the following questions:

1. According to Beyer, what are the three essential components of a family preservation program?
2. In the author's opinion, how should social workers base their judgments regarding the adequacy of a home?
3. What are the key components of a family preservation system for substance-abusing parents, as described by Beyer?

Reprinted from Margaret Beyer, "Too Little, Too Late: Designing Family Support to Succeed," New York University Review of Law & Social Change, vol. 22, no. 2 (1996), by permission of the publisher.

Removal of children from their families is the dominant response of legislatures and social service agencies when faced with the problem of maltreatment. However, the needs of many children are best served when they are permitted to remain with their families. Implementing safe family preservation requires the provision of services building upon families' strengths to enable families to meet the needs of their children. [This] system of care cuts across the areas of child welfare, education, health, housing, mental health, substance abuse, and criminal justice. When properly formulated, it simultaneously builds on family strengths, preserves ties between children and families, and attends to needs that, if unmet, put children at risk.

This strengths/needs approach to services makes possible a genuine partnership between social workers, families, and children. Effective family support requires that services are designed with families. Moreover, such services must be sufficiently intensive to address the child's safety and attachment needs, and of a sufficient duration to have a lasting impact. Indeed, unless the family and the older children agree with service providers about their needs, little will change in their lives. . . .

REASONABLE EFFORTS MUST BE MADE TO PRESERVE FAMILIES

Officially, the removal of children as the primary response to neglect and abuse ended in 1980 with the enactment of the Adoption Assistance and Child Welfare Act. The Act requires state child welfare agencies to make "reasonable efforts" to maintain a child with her family or, if removal is necessary, to return the child safely to the family or arrange another permanent home. But anti-family policies and practices have died slowly.

Prior to the passage of the Act, child welfare agencies in the United States espoused a child rescue philosophy. Although well intentioned, child rescue allowed children to drift in foster care for years and ignored the harm of separating children from their families. In contrast, the Adoption Assistance and Child Welfare Act is based on a family preservation philosophy. According to Alice C. Shotton, "This philosophy has as its starting point the belief that a child's biological family is the placement of first preference and that 'reasonable efforts' must be made to preserve this family as long as the child is safe." Even if reasonable efforts to preserve the family fail and the child must be removed, reasonable efforts must be made to reunify the child with the family.

Even for child welfare workers who believe in family preservation, implementing the philosophy in their day-to-day practice has been difficult. Inadequate services, inflexible agency policies and disjointed funding streams are obstacles to family preservation.

Sixteen years after the passage of the Act, children continue to be subjected unnecessarily to the trauma of lengthy separation from their families. Many neglected or abused children removed from loving but overwhelmed parents could be safely protected in their own homes if agencies provided sufficient services. Children who must be temporarily removed from unsafe homes could be protected if placed with family members or friends while the reasons for their maltreatment are addressed rather than placed in unfamiliar foster homes. . . .

FAMILY DEFICITS SHOULD NOT BE EMPHASIZED

Emphasizing deficits pushes the family into an enduring defensiveness. For example, case plans will often contain a statement such as "Ms. Lawrence must attend parenting skills class." This is not an assessment of what Ms. Lawrence needs. The service required cannot be determined until the caseworker identifies the need that the service will meet. Instead, the plan should state, "A strength of Ms. Lawrence is that she shows affection for her children. But when she has to cope with their many demands by herself for long periods, she feels depleted, gets angry, and sometimes loses control of her anger. *Ms. Lawrence needs regular breaks from their demands* so she does not get so worn out." This particular need, once it is specified, would best be matched with a babysitter. If she is referred to a parenting skills class, Ms. Lawrence is likely to feel defensive. If she chooses not to attend the class, she may be accused of not caring about her children.

For family support to succeed, any plan purporting to meet the reasonable efforts requirement of the Adoption Assistance and Child Welfare Act must contain three essential components: (1) services must be based on the family's strengths and needs; (2) children and families must be involved in identifying their strengths and needs and in designing the required services; and (3) services must be regularly adjusted to ensure their effectiveness in meeting the child's and family's needs.

Child and family assessment should generate information to guide services to improve the fit between the child's needs and the family's responsiveness. This should include a description of the strengths of the extended family, attachments, problem solving skills, and community involvement. The process of identifying, with the family, what is required to meet the needs of the children should address, at a minimum, the following:

- What are the family's strengths?
- Who is the child attached to; what relationship(s) does the child have to a parent or other family members absent from home?
- What is the impact of the family's cultural orientation on child rearing?
- How does the family handle conflict between the needs of the child and the needs of the child's primary caretakers?
- How does the family respond to the child's disobedience?
- What environmental, employment, economic, health, and other stressors exist for the family?
- Do family members abuse substances and how specifically does this interfere with meeting the child's needs?
- What is the family's perception of help-seeking and intervention?
- What specifically put the child at risk, and why did the family not attend to those particular safety needs?

BUILDING PARTNERSHIPS WITH THE FAMILY

Reaching agreement with the family about its needs should start with the very first contact. The caseworker must begin to build a partnership with the family at once. In the author's experience, when the caseworker sees the family's strengths, understands why the child was not protected, and builds a partnership with the family so they can help at the beginning to ensure the child's safety, case outcome improves in comparison to risk assessment techniques that primarily identify parental deficits. Since professionals knowledgeable about child development and families may look at a child's needs differently, reaching agreement can be a time-consuming process. In the author's experience, this process of reaching genuine agreement about the child's needs results in more effective services and earlier, safe case closing.

By recognizing a family's strengths and listening to the family's own assessment of its needs, a caseworker empowers the family. A deficit approach, by contrast, puts family members on the defensive and erodes their trust. Reaching agreement with a family on their needs leads to their active involvement in crafting services and their taking responsibility for change. Instead of sending the family to a program to have something done to it, the message is: You have agreed on what you need. The services you have helped to plan will assist you in getting your needs met.

Reasonable efforts go beyond providing referrals to services.

A family support plan may fail for multiple reasons: the agency may not have properly identified the child's and family's needs; the family may not agree with the caregiver about its needs; the family may not believe the services will meet its needs; and/or the caregivers may be skeptical about the family's capacity to change.

Adjusting Services According to Family Needs

The process of empowering families requires that services be adjusted when a family does not follow through. As Carl J. Dunst, Carol M. Trivette, and Angela G. Deal write,

> [U]nmet family needs in basic areas such as nutrition, shelter, safety, health care, child care, and so forth negatively affect parents' health and well-being, which, in turn, decreases the probability that parents will carry out professionally prescribed interventions. . . . Thus, a family who [sic] fails to adhere to a professionally prescribed regimen may do so not because its members are resistant, uncooperative, or noncompliant, but because the family's circumstances steer behavior in other directions.

If parents fail to utilize services, they probably do not believe the services will help meet their needs. Labelling the family resistant obscures parents' legitimate reasons for not utilizing services. The family may lack transportation or may require child care. The family may also feel uncomfortable in agencies, in which case the caseworker should arrange for home-based services. Perhaps the family does not fully understand their child's needs or how to meet them. If the family does not become involved in services, the caseworker must ask the family again, "What services will help you to meet your children's needs?"

Many practitioners wonder whether they should bother assessing and reaching agreement with the family about a child's needs if the child's emotional needs cannot be met by existing outpatient services and her educational needs cannot be met by the local school. However, when the caseworker and family reach agreement about the child's educational, emotional, and other needs and specify the help necessary to meet those needs, new services are much more likely to be developed, sometimes in surprising ways. For instance, in the case of Ms. Lawrence, the mother might have been referred to a parenting skills class. However, she really needed a babysitter to go into the home, perhaps daily, to give Ms. Lawrence a regular break so she could make use of her strengths as a parent and not become so depleted that she would lose control of her anger. While perhaps not previously included in the local continuum of child welfare services, a variety of informal or contractual arrangements could be used to procure a reliable babysitter in the home, keeping the children safe and leaving their attachment to their mother undisturbed.

WORKING TOGETHER TO PROTECT CHILDREN

A strengths/needs approach to services requires a complex web of working partnerships to protect the child within the family or other placement. Individuals who know the family's and child's strengths and needs must be brought together in the design—not just the delivery—of services. These individuals may include the caseworker, the teacher, the therapist, the nurse, the parent's substance abuse counselor, and a member of the local church. All must work from a shared statement of strengths and needs with which the family agrees and all must be accountable for meeting those needs.

Instead of assuming children will be better off without parents who have maltreated them, practitioners must ask what it will take to keep the child safe and protect the child from the loss of her family. In most cases, families want to meet their children's needs. Abusive and chronically neglectful families are not hopeless. Agencies—with the active participation of families—must design coordinated, strengths/needs-based services to support families in keeping their children safe without disturbing their attachments.

THE ROLE OF CULTURE

Effective support for families in meeting the needs of their children requires an understanding of minimal adequacy. Minimal adequacy should be defined in terms of safety and attachment—not some concept of idealized family life. Differences among families in childrearing require that guidelines for minimally adequate homes be based on universal child development principles. Since cultural differences affect how families define nurturing, caseworkers must focus on whether the child's needs are met and not on how the family cares for the child.

For example, in one case, a pediatrician notified child welfare that a two-year-old was not vocalizing despite normal hearing. The pediatrician suspected the child's speech delay resulted from neglect by the child's deaf parents. The investigative worker found that the parents were teaching the child sign language so she could communicate in their world. The parents resented outside intervention, but the pediatrician persisted because of her belief in a developmental window after which a child cannot easily learn to speak and in the necessity for a hearing child to be prepared to communicate in the hearing world. The caseworker enlisted the assistance of a hearing-impaired social worker from a school for the deaf. The social worker helped the parents recognize as unfounded their fear that the child would reject them or their deaf culture if she learned to speak by attending preschool with hearing children.

CONFUSING POVERTY WITH NEGLECT

By all accounts, at least half the children in foster care have never been maltreated by their parents. They have been removed from their homes solely because their parents are poor. The child welfare bureaucracy evinces a pernicious tendency to confuse poverty with child neglect, probably because case workers' checklists tend to define "deprivation of necessities" in material rather than emotional terms.

Dana Mack, *Los Angeles Times*, December 1, 1997.

This child's family demonstrates how a culture defines nurturing. Most families repeat the practices they experienced as children and will refuse to implement unfamiliar nurturing approaches that challenge the integrity of the family. If family members believe that adopting new methods will make the child unlike the family, they may feel too threatened to make the recommended changes, even if they have been told the changes are necessary for the child's health or cognitive or social development.

Minimally adequate nurturing guidelines must recognize that most families want the best for their children and that this includes keeping the children within the culture of the family. Applying a reasonable and accountable minimally adequate home standard requires reaching agreement with parents regarding their children's needs as well as how to monitor developmental milestones. Effective support helps families meet their children's needs in ways consistent with their particular culture and nurturing style.

DEFINING MINIMALLY ADEQUATE HOMES

Reaching agreement on universal child development requirements may prove difficult, as illustrated by the following case. The police and media were flooded with complaints about a father living in a van with his small children. As the caseworker summarized the situation, the community felt that "child welfare should not allow children to live like that." Essentially, the public felt that all children should be raised in "a nice home." However, no clear-cut standards for normal child-rearing practices exist.

Many children are raised in less than optimal environments for child development. The standard for minimally adequate homes should be determined by the nurturing a child needs. Minimally adequate nurturing must be defined in a developmental context because the conditions that would cause an infant to be physically or developmentally impaired are different than those for an older child.

Practitioners should base judgments regarding the adequacy of a home on whether the child's need for safety (defined as assurance of health and protection from physical danger) and caring (defined as demonstration of love and attention) are met. A family need not adhere to predetermined child-rearing techniques; the family must only provide safety and caring for its children. In many cases, alternate caretakers in the extended family or in-home service providers can be relied upon to meet the child's immediate needs for caring and safety. Thus, an effective intervention involves the following: identifying loving and protective individuals in the household; ensuring that they understand the child's needs for caring and safety; obtaining the agreement of one or more family members, in collaboration with the parents where possible, to take specified steps to meet the child's needs; and checking to ascertain that the child's needs are being met. . . .

DEALING WITH SUBSTANCE-ABUSING FAMILIES

Many parents who abuse or neglect their children are substance abusers. Substance abuse may lead to an angry assault on children, of which the parent has no memory the next day. Substance abuse may also reduce a person's inhibitions against incest. Although substance abusers may feel guilty about their behavior, they may be unaware of their children's needs. Typically, parents abuse alcohol or drugs in response to stress; they do not realize that they are gratifying their own needs before meeting their children's needs. Moreover, substance abuse becomes the organizer for the entire family; family members cover up and respond to the abuser's dependency.

Addiction is a chronic disease with a slow recovery process. Some individuals are incapable of controlled use and must abstain. Nevertheless, substance-abusing parents can be successfully supported to meet the needs of their children. Substance-abusing parents often require assistance to improve their responsiveness to their children, avoid over-stimulation of their children, and learn proper discipline techniques.

SUBSTANCE-ABUSING PARENTS CAN BE SUPPORTED

Supporting substance-abusing parents to meet the needs of their children requires an interagency approach that resolves the philosophical differences between family preservation and chemical dependency treatment. Substance-abuse workers might believe a child would be better off away from an abusing family. Substance-abuse counselors have often complained to this author that intervention by child welfare workers enables the parents' addiction and the family's co-dependency. Neighborhood-based interagency efforts can help create sober communities supportive of parenting in cases where the constant pressures of drugs and alcohol previously made family preservation impossible. With the proper services, families are able to recognize the degree to which their use of alcohol or drugs impairs the nurturing of their children.

Services must be sufficiently intensive to ensure that children are safe. One program for crack-using parents significantly reduced safety risks for children and improved their care by intensive (five to twenty hours weekly) in-home family services: 75% of the parents maintained sobriety for a twelve-month period after treatment. Motivated to keep their children, substance-abusing parents who receive sufficient services to have their children safely at home are more likely to persevere in treatment programs. . . .

Most families can meet their children's safety and attachment needs. Pro-family strengths/needs-based services capitalize on family strengths, preserve the children's attachments to their families, and address needs that, if unmet, put children at risk. Agencies can successfully design family support if they craft services with families, use the concept of minimally adequate homes to guide those implementing services, tailor services to meet individual needs, particularly those of substance-abusing families, and provide reunification services that address the risks causing removal and children's and parents' feelings about separation. While too little assistance provided too late puts children at risk, support services designed to succeed would enable most families to protect and meet the needs of their children.

"Family preservation's upbeat rhetoric
of 'respect for families'. . . masks
how deeply troubled those 'families'
really are."

FAMILY PRESERVATION PROGRAMS
PUT CHILDREN AT RISK

Heather MacDonald

In the following viewpoint, Heather MacDonald argues against
the validity of family preservation programs, which attempt to
keep families together after incidents of child abuse while working to change parents' abusive behavior. She asserts that family
preservation places children at risk and is little more than a
"quick fix" for dysfunctional families. Furthermore, MacDonald
contends, the optimistic philosophy behind family preservation
disregards the fact that some parents do not have the values or
means necessary for raising children. MacDonald is a contributing editor at the Manhattan Institute's *City Journal*, a magazine addressing urban issues in New York City.

As you read, consider the following questions:

1. According to MacDonald, what is the "guiding belief" of
   family preservation?
2. What, in the author's opinion, is the most significant
   ideological effect of family preservation?
3. What does the author offer as alternatives to family
   preservation?

Reprinted with permission of the author from Heather MacDonald, "The Ideology of
'Family Preservation,'" *The Public Interest*, no. 115 (Spring 1994), pp. 45–60, © 1994 by
National Affairs, Inc.

Can a single welfare mother who has been beating her children, or failing to feed and bathe them, be turned into a responsible parent as the result of a one-to-three month infusion of counselling, free food, cash, furniture, rent vouchers, and housekeeping services—all at public expense? The federal government and over thirty states think so. They have all embraced the hottest new trend in child welfare policy known as "family preservation."

"Family preservation" aims to decrease the number of children placed in foster care by quickly teaching their abusing or neglectful parents the skills necessary to keep the family together. It has transformed the child welfare field, but its significance extends far beyond that field. Family preservation embraces a non-judgmental ethic of support for all "families," carefully drawing no distinction between single- and two-parent households. It stands for the proposition that nearly all families, no matter how dysfunctional or abusive, can be put right with the proper mix of therapy and social services. The movement thus lies at the intersection of two critical areas in social policy: family values and family structure, and the problems of the underclass. . . .

FEATURES OF FAMILY PRESERVATION

Family preservation has several features which distinguish it from traditional social welfare services. Most important, it is short-term. The Homebuilders model, the prototype for all family preservation programs, averages about 6 weeks; the longest family preservation programs last up to three months. Family preservation is based on "crisis-intervention" theory, which holds that personal crises offer a heightened opportunity for behavioral change. Once the crisis is over, so, too, it is thought, is the opportunity for change, so short-term therapy is considered as beneficial as long-term.

Secondly, family preservation is intensive and home-based. Ideally, family preservation workers work with only two or three families at a time. They visit their clients several times a week and are on call twenty-four hours a day. In addition to providing counselling, social workers are authorized to offer numerous "hard" services, including cash, food, assistance with advocacy groups, rent vouchers, furniture, and housekeeping help.

Thirdly, the movement embodies an optimistic, tolerant attitude toward both family structure and family functioning. Says Robert Little, head of the Child Welfare Administration in New York City under former Mayor David Dinkins: "Family preservation is about a new set of values that guide how we perceive the problem. It argues that all families have strengths as well as weaknesses." The threshold for what qualifies as a "strength" for purposes of family preservation is rather low: merely having stayed together as a family is now viewed as a positive achievement. In addition, family preservation adopts what Richard Gelles, Director of the Family Violence Research Program at the University of Rhode Island, calls a "compassionate approach to maltreatment." It views abusive parents, Gelles says, as victims themselves. It sees the cause of child abuse and neglect in the personal history and current circumstances of the abuser, not in the character of the abuser himself.

WHEN IS FAMILY PRESERVATION IMPLEMENTED?

Family preservation services kick in when a child welfare agency determines both that a family is about to lose a child to foster care and that the child can be kept at home during the course of therapy without risk of injury. A typical crisis triggering the risk of placement in the original Homebuilders program in Washington was a parental threat to turn an unmanageable adolescent over to juvenile court. Other triggering crises could include the loss of a job or of housing or a sudden change in family structure. The family preservation worker acts as a jack-of-all-trades, offering the family not only therapy but also logistical and material help—buying groceries, weatherproofing windows, calling a plumber, taking the parent to appointments. The worker tries to help the family find positive ways of resolving its problems through "rational emotive therapy," a technique for teaching people how not to be controlled by their emotions. . . .

A "QUICK FIX"

The child welfare clientele . . . has become a population characterized by endemic substance abuse and weakened extended family. The typical neglectful family of the late '80s and early '90s possesses pervasive emotional and behavioral problems and is crippled in its abilities to compete in society. Such families are firmly set in a downward spiral; their problems seem to defy all notions of a "quick fix."

Yet a quick fix is precisely what family preservation aims to give such families. Though the problems that lead to foster care placement in the inner city bear little resemblance to the emotional crises that originally gave rise to family preservation techniques, the response is identical. Family preservation proceeds as if all its clients faced an acute crisis that can be resolved with short-term therapy and material aid. But child neglect today is typically chronic and all-pervasive, affecting not just physical care but also cognitive stimulation and emotional nurturance. The typical neglectful family is recalcitrant to treatment: the pattern of neglect is very apt to survive an agency's intervention. Indeed, in one study of chronically dysfunctional families, maltreatment continued right through the therapy for half the cases studied.

SACRIFICING CHILDREN

No doubt if you take a thousand children away from repeatedly abusive parents, somewhere among those thousand there may be one parent who would have straightened up and come to his or her senses, treating the child better in the future. But are you prepared to sacrifice 999 other children on the altar to this slim hope?

Thomas Sowell, *Conservative Chronicle*, July 2, 1997.

The very designation of family preservation's clients as "families" and the upbeat philosophy of tolerance and optimism that accompanies that designation may also be misplaced. In lieu of "family," some scholars in the field prefer the term "family fragments" to designate the mother-child groupings that are forever moving in and out of combination with boyfriends, aunts, cousins, and grandmothers. Yet the theories underlying most forms of family therapy assume a two-parent household or at least a stable one-parent family.

Even some of family preservation's proponents admit that there may be a discrepancy between the cure and the disease. James Whittaker of the University of Washington School of Social Work has written extensively in favor of family preservation but he acknowledges that parents who are neglectful—especially where drugs are involved—are one of family preservation's "greatest challenges," because they don't fit the traditional "family-in-conflict" model.

LOSING SIGHT OF THE CHILDREN

Despite these misgivings, family preservation has had a profound effect on the rhetoric and practice of child welfare. It is now widely understood that the mission of child welfare agencies is to "keep families together." Placing a child in foster care is now regarded as a sign of agency failure, even though it may represent the best interests of the child. Says William Grinker, head of the Human Resources Administration in New York City under former Mayor Edward Koch: "When family preservation becomes the centerpiece of a child welfare agency, especially in a large system like New York's with inexperienced, poorly trained workers, you begin to lose sight of the most important thing: to protect the child." The assumption that families are inevitably nurturing is now applied even in cases of serious physical and sexual abuse, which is often committed by stepparents and boyfriends who share no biological tie with the child.

If a child is removed to foster care, the ethic of family preservation insures that he will soon be returned home regardless of the circumstances. Edna Negron, principal of an elementary school in one of Hartford, Connecticut's toughest neighborhoods, told the Hartford Courant: "We have had kids in beautiful foster homes put back into homes that are completely dysfunctional. The mother gets out of jail, she's still drug addicted. Boom, the children are [sent] home, until she's rearrested." One-third of children discharged to their homes from foster care return within six months.

It has become almost impossible to free children for adoption because of the emphasis on family preservation. Mary Beth Seader, a vice president at the National Council for Adoption, complains: "I know people who have been trying for two years to adopt these crack babies that have been abandoned in hospitals, but . . . the state is not terminating parental rights even if there is no contact with the biological mother."

HORROR STORIES

Illinois's Family First program is an example of the myopia that can beset a determined family preservation bureaucracy. Six children have died during or just after family preservation; many more were injured or subjected to continuing neglect. A selection of some of their histories suggests the enormous mismatch between the social services offered and the problems they purport to address:

The case of Senomia B. is typical of the casualties. Her aunt had reported that the three-year-old girl was being abused by her mother and mother's boyfriend. From December, 1991 to March, 1992, social workers and housekeepers made thirty-seven visits to the home. They took Senomia's mother out to dinner seven times to discuss child-rearing with her in a "non-threatening environment." On March 17, 1992 the Illinois Department of Children and Family Services closed the case with a glowing report on how well the family was doing. Several hours later, Senomia was dead. She was brought to the emergency room with forty-three scars and burns on her body, most of which had been administered during the course of therapy. Her vagina and anus had been completely burned off by scalding water.

In spring of 1993, a drug-abusing mother was given family preservation services after having been charged with criminal battery of her two-year-old daughter. The authorities investigating the battery charge had found the girl and her eight-month-old brother eating out of dishes encrusted with rotten food and swarming with flies. Five days after family preservation services began, the boy was dead. Apparently the girl had tried to bathe him while the mother slept, leaving them unattended.

At the time of Patricia Brown's arrest in 1991 for prostituting her eleven-year-old daughter in exchange for heroin, money, and—once—a pair of athletic shoes, she had had a homemaker in her home four times a week for over a year as part of the Family First program. The police found Brown strung out on heroin and the children living in filth. Despite the recent services, the apartment had no running water, no electricity, no stove or refrigerator, no food for the children, no furniture except for an old mattress, and the toilet was overflowing with human waste. . . .

IDEOLOGICAL FUNCTIONS OF FAMILY PRESERVATION

The unopposed success of family preservation, despite its nonexistent empirical grounding, cannot be explained solely on the basis of its fiscal promises. Family preservation has succeeded in part because it plays an important ideological role in the culture's flight from honesty about the problems of the underclass. Its optimistic message that short-term therapy can mend the most dysfunctional of families papers over the social pathologies that are preventing stable families from forming in the first place.

Ideology is no stranger to the field of child welfare. Thousands of black children remain in limbo in foster care because the National Association of Black Social Workers has declared transracial adoptions to be a form of "cultural genocide." The genocide theme appears in discussions of foster care as well. Foster care is said to raise primal fears in blacks from the days of slavery. The overrepresentation of blacks in the child welfare system is attributed to racism on the part of child welfare workers and the courts, even though most child welfare workers in big cities are black. The Edna McConnell Clark Foundation argues that the presence of alleged child abuse may sometimes simply reflect cultural diversity: "'Abuse' may include errors of judgment or propriety that may reflect a group's cultural norms but violate standards of child protection experts or legislators."

The most important ideological effect of family preservation is to legitimate illegitimacy. Even though the proportion of single mothers in family preservation programs is extremely high—85 percent in Kentucky, 80 percent in Detroit, for example—and though neglect is found disproportionately in single parent households, family preservation studiously avoids any suggestion that there might be a connection between illegitimacy and family pathologies. Rather, the role of family preservation, according to the Clark Foundation, is to counsel the abusing or neglectful single mother "to the point of self-acceptance, so that she understands that she and her children are a valid family, too." A family preservation worker in a 1992 Bill Moyers TV special on family preservation decries the "labelling process" that puts a family with two working parents who can't afford day care in a "different category" from a single mother on crack who is neglecting her children. "If we're a country that believes in the integrity of families," the worker intones, "we should keep all families together."

Family preservation's upbeat rhetoric of "respect for families" and for "cultural diversity" also masks how deeply troubled those "families" really are. Such denial is pervasive throughout the child welfare system. Mothers with fourteen to sixteen confirmed neglect reports are still sent to "parenting" and "anger" classes. After duly collecting their completion forms, they are reported again in six weeks.

A LACK OF VALUES

Family preservation translates deficits of values into deficits of resources—the maltreating parent does not necessarily lack the values to raise a child responsibly, it is argued, but simply the resources to do so. Once so defined, the problem is ripe for intervention from the massive social service bureaucracy.

The charge that social workers "mistake poverty for neglect" is central to the shift from a focus on values to one on resources. In a typical antidote to such "insensitivity," Illinois has signed a consent decree agreeing not to remove a child from a family that is failing to provide for the child's subsistence needs unless the state itself makes "reasonable efforts" to meet those needs. "Reasonable efforts" is defined as providing temporary shelter, assistance in locating and securing housing, cash, in-kind services including food and clothing, child care, emergency caretakers, and advocacy with public agencies. Left out of the analysis is why the family is not providing for the child—might not drugs or sheer irresponsibility play a more important role than poverty?

That question is now taboo. The failure to ask it leads to ever more ludicrous government behavior. A deranged man in Chicago tore apart his entire home, stripping it of plumbing and electrical pipes. The children were living in the basement and using a kitchen pot for a toilet. The Illinois Department of Children and Family Services investigated the case for reported child neglect and decided that the family's problem was inadequate housing. The department paid for the family to move into a new apartment and bought them new furniture.

FAMILY AUTONOMY

Family preservation claims to stand for family autonomy against unwarranted state intrusion. Yet its nonjudgmental approach to family formation leads to just the opposite result: a growing number of "families" who can survive only with constant state support. Some family preservation advocates cheerfully contemplate a nearly complete shifting of long-term responsibility for child care from certain families to the state. Brenda McGowan, professor of social work at Columbia University, acknowledges the discrepancy between family preservation's assumptions and the reality of underclass families:

> What is often ignored in the rush to institutionalize these services is the fact that they are based on a crisis intervention model, which assumes the capacity for independent functioning once balance is restored. Unfortunately, not all parents have the emotional, cognitive, social or economic resources necessary to enable them to function independently on a consistent basis.

But McGowan responds by extending further the flawed premise that therapy and state support can solve all problems: "[These families] can maintain loving homes and meet their children's basic development needs only if they are provided a range of supports on a sustained basis, perhaps until their children are grown."

But a "family" that from day one stands no chance at self-sufficiency probably should not have been conceived in the first place. There is no evidence that social services can compensate for the lack of personal responsibility that is fueling America's epidemic of illegitimacy. Teen-age pregnancy has more than doubled in the last fifteen years, to 1.2 million births annually; in the near future one in three babies will be born to a single mother. As Peter Rossi has argued: "Once the mother has the child, the fundamental irresponsibility has already been committed. There is an awesome amount of neglect: that is the main thing. The notion that you can deal with it by therapy and cash is ludicrous."

ALTERNATIVES TO FAMILY PRESERVATION

A percentage of troubled families do just need a helping hand to get through a crisis. For them, short-term intensive services may indeed be appropriate. But for the children of parents who wholly lack the emotional resources to raise a family, the foster care system should be improved. Foster parents could be better trained. Group foster homes could be saved by giving back to their directors the authority to enforce discipline and responsibility, tools long since taken away by child welfare advocates. And both the letter and the spirit of adoption policy should be changed to encourage more adoptions, no matter what the race of the child.

In the long run, however, as long as we keep circling around the issue of values and personal responsibility, we will continue devising costly solutions to family problems that are doomed to fail. The child welfare system is not working because it is the wrong answer to the problems of illegitimacy and social dysfunction.

Periodical Bibliography

The following articles have been selected to supplement the diverse views presented in this chapter. Addresses are provided for periodicals not indexed in the *Readers' Guide to Periodical Literature*, the *Alternative Press Index*, the *Social Sciences Index*, or the *Index to Legal Periodicals and Books*.

Jim Breig	"Labeling Sex Offenders Won't Protect Children," *U.S. Catholic*, November 1996.
Mubarak S. Dahir	"Sudden Visibility," *Advocate*, April 15, 1997.
Peter Davis	"The Sex Offender Next Door," *New York Times Magazine*, July 28, 1996.
Midge Decter	"Megan's Law and the 'New York Times,'" *Commentary*, October 1994.
Don Feder	"Parent Licensing Assaults Citadel of Civilization," *Conservative Chronicle*, October 26, 1994. Available from 9 Second St. NW, Hampton, IA 50441.
William Norman Grigg	"Whose Children? America's Parents Are Battling for the Right to Raise Their Kids," *New American*, July 21, 1997. Available from 770 Westhill Blvd., Appleton, WI 54914.
Albert R. Hunt	"Abused Kids Get Squeezed by the Ideologues," *Wall Street Journal*, February 27, 1997.
Issues and Controversies On File	"Sex-Offender Notification," July 26, 1996. Available from Facts On File News Services, 11 Penn Plaza, New York, NY 10001-2006.
Alexandra Dylan Lowe	"New Laws Put Kids First," *ABA Journal*, May 1996.
David T. Lykken	"Psychopathy, Sociopathy, and Crime," *Society*, November/December 1996.
Dennis Saffran	"Fatal Preservation," *City Journal*, Summer 1997. Available from 52 Vanderbilt Ave., New York, NY 10017.
Thomas Sowell	"Saving Children from Rotten Parents," *Conservative Chronicle*, July 2, 1997.
Update	"Public Notification of Sex Offenders," January 1995. Available from the American Prosecutors Research Institute, 99 Canal Center Plaza, Suite 510, Alexandria, VA 22314.

FOR FURTHER DISCUSSION

CHAPTER 1

1. The authors of this chapter present five different causes of child abuse. Whose argument is strongest? Why? Which factor do you think contributes most to child abuse?

2. On what basis does Murray A. Straus argue that spanking is dangerous to children under any circumstance? How might you refute his assertion that parents should never spank their children?

3. All of the authors of this chapter discuss, to varying degrees, the role of parents in causing child abuse. Identify how each author attributes child abuse to parents.

CHAPTER 2

1. Leora N. Rosen and Michelle Etlin contend that the child protection system (CPS) does not pursue suspicions of child abuse aggressively enough. Armin A. Brott criticizes the child protection system for the opposite reason, claiming that CPS's overzealous approach to investigating child abuse has led to an explosion in false accusations. Whose argument do you find more convincing, and why? How do these authors' contrasting views on the prevalence of child abuse influence their beliefs about the appropriate role of the child protection system?

2. Hans Sebald maintains that children's accounts of child sexual abuse cannot be trusted. In arguing that children lie about sexual abuse, what assumptions does Sebald make about children? What assumptions does he make about adults? Do you agree with these assumptions? Why or why not?

3. Elizabeth Loftus refers to memories of child sexual abuse that are recalled later in life as "false memories," whereas Jennifer J. Freyd calls them "recovered memories." How do these terms reflect Loftus's and Freyd's opposing views on the issue of whether memories of child sexual abuse are valid?

CHAPTER 3

1. The authors of this chapter discuss three different proposals for how child molesters should be dealt with: rehabilitation, castration, and detention in mental institutions. List the advantages and disadvantages of each proposal. Which method of dealing with child molesters would be most effective? Explain your answer.

2. The question of whether child molesters can be successfully rehabilitated has elicited much controversy. Eric Lotke provides statistics that document the success of psychological treatment programs in rehabilitating child molesters. Do these statistics convince you that child molesters should be released back into society? Why or why not?

3. Samuel Francis contends that detaining child molesters indefinitely in mental institutions defies the Fifth Amendment, which states that "no person shall be . . . subject for the same offence to be twice put in jeopardy of life or limb." Do you agree with Francis's assertion that detaining child molesters in mental institutions after they have served jail time infringes on their constitutional right to not be punished twice for the same crime? In your opinion, should criminals such as child molesters have the same rights as other citizens? Why or why not?

Chapter 4

1. In an attempt to help parents protect their children from sex offenders, community notification legislation—laws that require communities to be notified of the presence of convicted child molesters—has been enacted on the state and federal level. What reasons does Elizabeth Schroeder give for the abolition of such laws? Do you think her objections outweigh parents' right to know about potential threats to their children? Explain your answer.

2. Jack C. Westman contends that requiring a minimum standard for parenting would reduce child abuse significantly. William Norman Grigg, on the other hand, objects to parental licensure on the grounds that it allows the government to assume authority that should be left to individuals. According to Westman and Grigg, what role should the government play in reducing child abuse? Do you think that parent licensing would infringe upon individuals' right to reproduce? Defend your answer, using evidence from the viewpoints.

3. According to Margaret Beyer, family preservation programs benefit children by keeping them with their biological parents and working with the parents to prevent further incidents of abuse. Heather MacDonald refutes Beyer's argument, claiming that keeping abusive families together puts children at risk of more abuse. How do Beyer's and MacDonald's differing views of what constitutes a family reflect their attitudes about family preservation? Whose argument do you find more persuasive, and why?

ORGANIZATIONS TO CONTACT

The editors have compiled the following list of organizations concerned with the issues debated in this book. The descriptions are derived from materials provided by the organizations. All have publications or information available for interested readers. The list was compiled on the date of publication of the present volume; the information provided here may change. Be aware that many organizations take several weeks or longer to respond to inquiries, so allow as much time as possible.

ACT for Kids
7 S. Howard, Suite 200, Spokane, WA 99201-3816
(509) 747-8224 • fax: (509) 747-0609
e-mail: info@actforkids.org • web address: http://www.actforkids.org

ACT for Kids is a nonprofit organization that provides resources, consultation, research and training for the prevention and treatment of child abuse and sexual violence. The organization publishes workbooks, manuals, and books such as *My Very Own Book About Me* and *How to Survive the Sexual Abuse of Your Child*.

American Academy of Child and Adolescent Psychiatry (AACAP)
3615 Wisconsin Ave. NW, Washington, DC 20016-3007
(202) 966-7300 • fax: (202) 966-2891
web address: http://www.aacap.org

AACAP is a nonprofit organization that supports and advances child and adolescent psychiatry through research and the distribution of information. The academy's goal is to provide information that will remove the stigma associated with mental illnesses and assure proper treatment for children who suffer from mental or behavioral disorders due to child abuse, molestation, or other factors. AACAP publishes fact sheets on a variety of issues concerning disorders that may affect children and adolescents.

American Professional Society on the Abuse of Children (APSAC)
407 S. Dearborn, Suite 1300, Chicago, IL 60605
(312) 554-0166 • fax: (312) 554-0919
e-mail: APSACMems@aol.com • web address: http://www.apsac.org

APSAC is dedicated to improving the coordination of services in the fields of child abuse prevention, treatment, and research. It publishes a quarterly newsletter, the *Advisor*, and the *Journal of Interpersonal Violence*.

False Memory Syndrome Foundation
3401 Market St., Suite 130, Philadelphia, PA 19104-3315
(215) 387-1865 • (800) 568-8882 • fax: (215) 387-1917
e-mail: pjf@saul.cis.upenn.edu

The foundation believes that many "delayed memories" of sexual abuse are the result of false memory syndrome (FMS). In FMS, patients in therapy "recall" childhood abuse that never occurred. The foundation seeks to discover reasons for the spread of FMS, works for the prevention of new cases, and aids FMS victims, including those falsely accused of abuse. The foundation publishes a newsletter and various papers and distributes articles and information on FMS.

Federation on Child Abuse and Neglect
134 S. Swan St., Albany, NY 12210
(518) 445-1273 • (800) CHILDREN (244-5373)
web address: http://www.childabuse.org
(National Committee to Prevent Child Abuse website)

Created by the National Committee to Prevent Child Abuse, the federation is dedicated to preventing child abuse by raising public awareness about the causes and prevention of abuse. It also advocates legislation and programs that aim to protect children from abuse. The federation offers brochures such as *What Kids Should Know About Child Abuse and Neglect*, booklets such as *Child Sexual Abuse Guidelines for Health Professionals*, fact sheets, and reprinted articles.

King County Sexual Assault Resource Center (KCSARC)
PO Box 300, Renton, WA 98057
(206) 226-5062 • fax: (206) 235-7422

KCSARC provides crisis intervention, counseling, consultation, and legal assistance to victims and survivors of child sexual abuse, incest, and sexual assault. The program also provides training for teachers, parents, and other professionals who work with children. KCSARC publishes the newsletters *Outlook* and *Teen Talk* as well as a variety of resources including videos, books, and pamphlets.

National Center for Missing & Exploited Children (NCMEC)
2101 Wilson Blvd., Arlington, VA 22201-3077
(703) 235-3900 • fax: (703) 235-4067
hot line: (800) THE-LOST (843-5678)
web address: http://www.missingkids.org

NCMEC serves as a clearinghouse of information on missing and exploited children and coordinates child protection efforts with the private sector. A number of publications on these issues are available, including guidelines for parents whose children are testifying in court, help for abused children, and booklets such as *Children Traumatized in Sex Rings* and *Child Molesters: A Behavioral Analysis*.

National Clearinghouse on Child Abuse and Neglect Information
PO Box 1182, Washington, DC 20013-1182
(703) 385-7565 • (800) 394-3366 • fax: (703) 385-3206
e-mail: nccanch@calib.com
web address: http://www.calib.com/nccanch

This national clearinghouse collects, catalogs, and disseminates information on all aspects of child maltreatment, including identification, prevention, treatment, public awareness, training, and education. The clearinghouse offers various reports, fact sheets, and bulletins concerning child abuse and neglect.

National Coalition Against Domestic Violence (NCADV)
Child Advocacy Task Force
PO Box 18749, Denver, CO 80218-0749
(303) 839-1852 • fax: (303) 831-9251
web address: http://www.ncadv.org

NCADV represents organizations and individuals that assist battered women and their children. The Child Advocacy Task Force deals with issues affecting children who witness violence at home or are themselves abused. It publishes the *Bulletin*, a quarterly newsletter.

National Committee to Prevent Child Abuse (NCPCA)
332 S. Michigan Ave., Suite 1600, Chicago, IL 60604-4357
(312) 663-3520 • fax: (312) 939-8962
e-mail: ncpca@childabuse.org
web address: http://www.childabuse.org

NCPCA's mission is to prevent all forms of child abuse. It distributes and publishes materials on a variety of topics, including child abuse and child abuse prevention. *Talking About Child Sexual Abuse* and *You Don't Have to Molest That Child* are among the various pamphlets NCPCA offers.

National Criminal Justice Reference Service (NCJRS)
U.S. Department of Justice
PO Box 6000, Rockville, MD 20849-6000
(301) 519-5500 • (800) 851-3420
e-mail: askncjrs@ncjrs.org • web address: http://www.ncjrs.org

NCJRS is a research and development agency of the U.S. Department of Justice established to prevent and reduce crime and to improve the criminal justice system. Among its publications are *Resource Guidelines: Improving Court Practice in Child Abuse and Neglect Cases* and *Recognizing When a Child's Injury or Illness Is Caused by Abuse.*

The Safer Society Foundation
PO Box 340-I, Brandon, VT 05733-0340
(802) 247-3132 • fax: (802) 247-4233
e-mail: ray@usa-ads.net • web address: http://www.safersociety.org

The Safer Society Foundation is a national research, advocacy, and referral center for the prevention of sexual abuse of children and adults. The Safer Society Press publishes research, studies, and books on treatment for sexual victims and offenders and on the prevention of sexual abuse.

Survivor Connections
52 Lyndon Rd., Cranston, RI 02905-1121
(401) 941-2548 • fax: (401) 941-2335
e-mail: scsitereturn@hotmail.com
web address: http://www.angelfire.com/ri/survivorconnections/

Survivor Connections is an activist center for survivors of incest, rape, sexual assault, and child molestation. It publishes the *Survivor Activist*, a newsletter available through regular mail.

United Fathers of America (UFA)

6360 Van Nuys Blvd., Suite 8, Van Nuys, CA 91401
(818) 785-1440 • fax: (818) 995-0743
e-mail: info@unitedfathers.com
web address: http://www.fathersunited.com
web address: http://www.fathersforever.com (a branch of UFA)

UFA helps fathers fight for the right to remain actively involved in their children's upbringing after divorce or separation. UFA believes that children should not be subject to the emotional and psychological trauma caused when vindictive parents falsely charge ex-spouses with sexually abusing their children. Primarily a support group, UFA answers specific questions and suggests articles and studies that illustrate its position.

VOCAL/National Association of State VOCAL Organizations (NASVO)

4584 Appleton Ave., Jacksonville, FL 32210
hot line: (303) 233-5321 • fax: (904) 381-7097
e-mail: vocal@vocal.org • web address: http://www.vocal.org

VOCAL (Victims of Child Abuse Laws) provides information, research data, referrals, and emotional support for those who have been falsely accused of child abuse. NASVO maintains a library of research on child abuse and neglect issues, focusing on legal, mental health, social, and medical issues, and will provide photocopies of articles for a fee. It publishes the bimonthly newsletter *NASVO News*.

BIBLIOGRAPHY OF BOOKS

Louise Armstrong — Rocking the Cradle of Sexual Politics: What Happened When Women Said Incest. Reading, MA: Addison-Wesley, 1994.

C. Brooks Brenneis — Recovered Memories of Trauma: Transferring the Present to the Past. Madison, CT: International Universities Press, 1997.

Vern L. Bullough and Bonnie Bullough — Sexual Attitudes: Myths and Realities. Amherst, NY: Prometheus Books, 1995.

Mukti Jain Campion — Who's Fit to Be a Parent? London: Routledge, 1995.

Stephen J. Ceci and Maggie Bruck — Jeopardy in the Courtroom: A Scientific Analysis of Children's Testimony. Washington, DC: American Psychological Association, 1995.

Center for the Future of Children — Sexual Abuse of Children. Los Altos, CA: The Center, 1994.

Dante Cicchetti and Vicki K. Carlson, eds. — Theory and Research on the Causes and Consequences of Child Abuse and Neglect. Cambridge, MA: Cambridge University Press, 1989.

Lela B. Costin, Howard Jacob Karger, and David Stoesz — The Politics of Child Abuse in America. New York: Oxford University Press, 1996.

Lisa Aronson Fontes, ed. — Breaking the Silences: Considering Culture in Child Sexual Abuse. Newbury Park, CA: Sage, 1995.

Jennifer J. Freyd — Betrayal Trauma: The Logic of Forgetting Childhood Abuse. Cambridge, MA: Harvard University Press, 1996.

Richard J. Gelles — The Book of David: How Preserving Families Can Cost Children's Lives. New York: BasicBooks, 1996.

Angelo Giardino, Cindy Christian, and Eileen R. Giardino — A Practical Guide to the Evaluation of Child Physical Abuse and Neglect. Thousand Oaks, CA: Sage, 1997.

Pat Gilmartin — Rape, Incest, and Child Sexual Abuse: Consequences and Recovery. New York: Garland, 1994.

Gail S. Goodman — Testifying in Criminal Court: Emotional Effects on Child Sexual Assault Victims. Chicago: University of Chicago Press, 1992.

Gordon C. Nagayama Hall — Theory-Based Assessment, Treatment, and Prevention of Sexual Aggression. New York: Oxford University Press, 1996.

Kathleen M. Heide — Why Kids Kill Parents: Child Abuse and Adolescent Homicide. Columbus: Ohio State University Press, 1992.

C. Ronald Huff, Arye Rattner, and Edward Sagarin	Convicted but Innocent: Wrongful Conviction and Public Policy. Thousand Oaks, CA: Sage, 1996.
Mic Hunter, ed.	Adult Survivors of Sexual Abuse: Treatment Innovations. Thousand Oaks, CA: Sage, 1995.
Valerie Jackson	Racism and Child Protection: The Black Experience of Child Sexual Abuse. London: Cassell, 1996.
Philip Jenkins	Pedophiles and Priests: Anatomy of a Contemporary Crisis. New York: Oxford University Press, 1996.
Karen L. Kinnear	Childhood Sexual Abuse: A Reference Handbook. Santa Barbara, CA: ABC-CLIO, 1995.
Caroline Knowles	Family Boundaries: The Invention of Normality and Dangerousness. Orchard Park, NY: Broadview Press, 1996.
Alex V. Levin and Mary S. Sheridan	Munchausen Syndrome by Proxy: Issues in Diagnosis and Treatment. San Francisco: Jossey-Bass, 1995.
Elizabeth F. Loftus and Katherine Ketcham	The Myth of Repressed Memory: False Memories and Allegations of Sexual Abuse. New York: St. Martin's Press, 1994.
Cloe Madanes et al.	The Violence of Men: New Techniques for Working with Abusive Families: A Therapy of Social Action. San Francisco: Jossey-Bass, 1995.
Debbie Nathan and Michael Snedeker	Satan's Silence: Ritual Abuse and the Making of a Modern American Witch Hunt. New York: BasicBooks, 1995.
National Institute of Justice	Childhood Victimization and Risk for Alcohol and Drug Arrests. Washington, DC: U.S. Dept. of Justice, Office of Justice Programs, 1995.
James Randall Noblitt and Pamela Sue Perskin	Cult and Ritual Abuse: Its History, Anthropology, and Recent Discovery in Contemporary America. Westport, CT: Praeger, 1995.
Joy D. Osofsky, ed.	Children in a Violent Society. New York: Guilford Press, 1997.
Kathy Pezdek and William P. Banks, eds.	The Recovered Memory/False Memory Debate. San Diego: Academic Press, 1996.
Douglas W. Pryor	Unspeakable Acts: Why Men Sexually Abuse Children. New York: New York University Press, 1996.
Leora N. Rosen	The Hostage Child: Sex Abuse Allegations in Custody Disputes. Bloomington: Indiana University Press, 1996.
Gail Ryan and Sandy Lane	Juvenile Sexual Offending. San Francisco: Jossey-Bass, 1997.
Inger A. Sagatun and Leonard P. Edwards	Child Abuse and the Legal System. Chicago: Nelson-Hall, 1995.

Barbara K. Schwartz and H.R. Cellini, eds.	*A Practitioner's Guide to Treating the Incarcerated Male Sex Offender.* Washington, DC: U.S. Dept. of Justice, National Institute of Corrections, 1988.
Murray A. Straus	*Beating the Devil Out of Them: Corporal Punishment in American Families.* New York: Lexington Books, 1994.
Carolyn F. Swift ed.	*Sexual Assault and Abuse: Sociocultural Context of Prevention.* New York: Haworth Press, 1995.
Lenore Terr	*Unchained Memories: True Stories of Traumatic Memories, Lost and Found.* New York: BasicBooks, 1994.
United States General Accounting Office	*Sex Offender Treatment: Research Results Inconclusive About What Works to Reduce Recidivism.* Washington, DC: The Office, 1996.
Claudette Wassil-Grimm	*Diagnosis for Disaster: The Devastating Truth About False Memory Syndrome and Its Impact on Accusers and Families.* Woodstock, NY: Overlook Press, 1995.
Charles L. Whitfield	*Memory and Abuse: Remembering and Healing the Effects of Trauma.* Deerfield Beach, FL: Health Communications, 1995.

INDEX